SUCCESS WITH

ALPINE GARDENING

GRAHAM CLARKE

SUCCESS WITH

ALPINE GARDENING

GRAHAM CLARKE

THE GUILD OF MASTER CRAFTSMAN PUBLICATIONS

First published 2010 by
Guild of Master Craftsman Publications Ltd
166 High Street, Lewes, East Sussex BN7 1XU

Text © Graham Clarke, 2010
© Copyright in the Work, GMC Publications Ltd, 2010

ISBN 978-1-86108-639-6

A catalogue record of this book is available
from the British Library.

Associate Publisher: Jonathan Bailey
Production Manager: Jim Bulley
Managing Editor: Gerrie Purcell
Senior Project Editor: Virginia Brehaut
Editor: Judith Chamberlain-Webber
Managing Art Editor: Gilda Pacitti
Design: Studio Ink

Photographic credits:
All pictures are by the author except for the following:

GMC/Eric Sawford: 28, 103, 104 (right), 105 (left), 106 (left),
107 (left), 108 (left), 109 (left), 111 (left), 113 (both), 116 (right),
117 (both), 119 (right), 120 (both), 121 (right), 123 (left), 125
(left), 129 (both), 132 (right), 133 (right), 134 (left), 135 (left),
136 (right), 137 (left), 139 (left), 141 (right), 142 (left), 146 (left),
154 (both) and 155 (left)
www.morguefile.com: 10, 11 (top and below left)
Hozelock: 50
Jupiter Greenhouses: 65 (top)
Alitex: 73
Flickr: 98

Colour origination: GMC Reprographics
Printed and bound: in Thailand by KNP

Previous page: In amongst the rocks
This Saxifraga 'Tysoe' nestles happily into the crevices of the rock.

Top: Large rocks
You do not need large rocks to make a successful rockery
feature – but they do help provide size, scale and supremacy.

Bottom: Alpine planting
Landscaping an area using alpine plants is fun and rewarding,
but you must make sure you have the right plants.

→ CONTENTS

Introduction — 6

Chapter 01
What are alpine plants? — 9

Chapter 02
How to use alpines in the garden — 19

Chapter 03
Buying alpine plants — 29

Chapter 04
Creating a rock garden — 37

Chapter 05
Alpines in containers — 55

Chapter 06
The alpine house — 63

Chapter 07
Year-round maintenance — 75

Chapter 08
A–Z directory of alpine plants — 99

Glossary — 156
Index — 157

INTRODUCTION

Rock gardening, and the cultivation of small plants whose natural habitats are high in the world's hills or mountains, has been one of the major innovations of recent horticulture. Like all specialist subjects, of course, it flows in and out in terms of popularity, but currently there seems little sign of slackening. In fact, interest in growing alpines seems to be increasing and this is almost certainly due to the fact that our gardens are getting smaller.

Land is being gobbled up by construction work of all sorts, from roads and transport networks, to industrial, office and large retail complexes. The maximum number of dwellings must, it seems, be squeezed into the minimum amount of space, and that means the average size of gardens is diminishing, often in alarming proportions. For example, the gardens attached to newly built properties can be as little as 322 sq ft (6 x 5m), and this is certainly not the smallest that may be found.

It is hardly surprising therefore that people are growing smaller plants. And this is where alpines come into their own. Luckily, the range of these small plants available on the market is huge. They can be very beautiful, they are full of interest and there is something for all tastes. Not only that, they are also plants that generally look after themselves: once planted they can usually be left to their own devices, making them perfect for the gardener who is short of time (as well as short of space).

There are two main parts to this book. In the first part we will look at the origins of alpine plants, how they have become a mainstay in our gardens, and also what to look for when buying them. The practical elements of ground preparation (and even the creation of a rockery garden) will be explained, followed by the very important elements of planting, nurturing and aftercare. Keeping alpine plants happy is not difficult, provided you follow a few basic rules.

Chapter 8 (starting on page 99), looks closely at some of the plants that are at the forefront of alpine gardening. The choice of available alpine plants has changed dramatically in the past 100 years. Before this, enthusiastic alpine gardeners would have had to grow species plants, propagated from subjects collected from the wild. Most of these plants would have produced brightly coloured flowers; this is because alpines growing in high crevices are often secluded from view, and in order to attract the all-important insect pollinators they needed flowers of the brightest possible colours.

It wasn't until the more sophisticated plant breeding of the twentieth century that we discovered the potential with alpines, and many subtler hues and pastel colours were introduced as a result. It means, of course, that the legacy for gardeners today is a massive choice ... and we hope that this is reflected in the directory of alpines in chapter 8.

Finally, do not for a moment believe that if you do not have a rock garden, you cannot grow alpine plants. You can – there are containers, sinks, pots and frames that can all accommodate a decorative and fascinating collection. If you have a well-ventilated, unheated greenhouse and a bed or border with space for a few rocks, then you're set for a fascinating and rewarding hobby.

→ **Creating a rock garden**
The range of alpine plants on the market today is such that enthusiasts can create the rock feature of their dreams.

01.

WHAT ARE ALPINE PLANTS?

Contemporary and colourful

Who said a rock garden has to have height, running water and emulate nature in all its glory? This contemporary garden uses alpine plants, flat stone and gravel to make a colourful feature.

THE ORIGINS OF 'ALPINE' PLANTS

Before you start imagining yourself up a mountain somewhere, wearing climbing boots and clinging on to an ice-pick, it is worth having a look at the derivation and usage of the word 'alpine'. It comes from the days when interest in mountain plants as good specimens for rockery gardens in the western world was high – some 150–200 years ago. Most of these plants actually came from the Alps, so not surprisingly became known as alpines.

Nowadays the word is certainly used to include plants from the Alps, but also every other mountainous and hilly region on the planet, as well as any plant that by its nature and habit just 'looks right' on a rock garden. Therefore, the term 'rock garden plant' is practically interchangeable with that of 'alpine'.

Plant collectors

After the influx of plants from the Alps, more followed from other European mountain ranges. Then plant hunters, who were explorers and botanists rolled into one, began to look further afield and soon brought back large collections of newly discovered plants from regions in the East, such as the Himalayas and the highlands around northern Burma as well as China and Tibet. Many of these plants turned out to be completely hardy and quickly became established in our gardens.

Further explorations as far as Japan, then back through India and to the Middle East and northern Africa, added to the increasingly rich diversity. The plant hunters then invaded the Americas and finally Australia and New Zealand were tapped for their rich seams of plant material.

South Africa was the last region to be explored, although many of the plants here have been deemed too tender to grow outside in cooler climes. But, to the resourceful alpine enthusiast, this just means that the plants need to be grown under cover.

↗ **Alpine panorama**
The Alps were the mountain range that offered early plant collectors its rich diversity of alpine plants.

↗ **Snow-covered peak**
The Eiger, one of the European mountains that has been host to a wide range of alpine plants.

↗ **Austrian mountains**
A sunny mountain slope in Austria – where a huge variety of vegetation grows.

↗ **Heather in snow**
For much of the year mountain plants, including heathers, in their natural habitat are covered with snow.

THE FIRST ROCKERIES

The plant hunters amassed alpine species of all sizes. The larger types were easily placed in the burgeoning botanical gardens of the nineteenth century, but the small plants – the like of which had not really been collected or studied before – needed a place to themselves, where they would not be invaded or overshadowed.

It was natural, therefore, to put these plants where they could be seen and admired. Because many were from high altitudes or had been found where rock formations abounded, the gardeners imported rock and stone to make the plants look at home. The real popularity of alpines took off after 1900; before this time there were very few true rock gardens in existence.

Just as there is debate over the terms 'alpine' and 'rock-garden plant', so too is there over 'rockery' and 'rock garden'. For enthusiasts today, the rockery is something of a mockery, while the term 'rock garden' suggests a serious approach to the subject, with a degree of knowledge and expertise. This was not always the case – by 1900 'rockeries' were becoming popular and respected features of domestic gardens.

Technically, however, they were frequently quite appalling by today's standards. They were often out of keeping with their surroundings, or inappropriate to the cultivation of the plants – or both. Usually the rockery consisted of a mound of soil, often in a shady or obscure part of the garden, and onto this mound would be strewn lumps of stone. There was little or no regard to making the area appear naturalistic, nor to its suitability or even its beauty.

→ **Random rocks**
Placing rocks in a haphazard way, as seen here, is risky as it could be very successful, or look awful!

COLOURFUL ROCKERY

A contemporary rockery, with rocks, plants and grit mulch placed strategically and geometrically, making no pretence of resembling nature. This works well as the gardener has skilfully chosen paving slabs and shingle that complement the planting.

Between the stones were pockets of soil, and this often would have been deep, fertile topsoil from elsewhere in the garden – just the sort of environment many alpine plants loathe. For this reason many of the choicer plants perished in what, for them, were inhospitable – and unnatural – conditions.

In addition, the mound could be large and quite difficult to tend, certainly as far as weeding and watering were concerned, so only the most durable plants survived. These were frequently the most vigorous as well.

The rock used was quite variable and in many cases did not fit in with either the local surroundings or with the types of plants being grown. It was also a common sight to see lumps of concrete being used when natural stone was not readily available.

Today, alpine enthusiasts know that if a garden is very formal in appearance or entirely flat, placing rocks in an attempt to imitate mountain terrain is both out of place and futile in an aesthetic sense. As we will discover, there are much better ways to grow alpines in flat gardens.

ALPINE TIP

To have a successful rock garden at home, you must be willing to give it the site and conditions that will promote success, and not to handicap yourself hopelessly from the start. Do not be tempted to put a rockery in a corner 'where nothing else will grow'.

ALPINE GROUPS

Generally, the most successful gardens are those where the plants grown are naturally suited or can adapt to the prevailing conditions of soil, situation and climate. This certainly applies to the cultivation of alpine plants. Although so many are adaptable, it stands to reason that those native to high alpine screes and moraines will need different conditions from those inhabiting woods, meadows, tundra or sandy banks at lower altitudes. And the same applies to latitudes where their long-standing habitat has put limits on their moisture requirement and degree of hardiness.

It follows on evolutionary principles that, as plants adapt themselves to the prevailing conditions in nature, the habit of growth shows wide variations. The term 'habit' has become accepted for describing the type of growth, and in alpines this falls into several sections.

↗ **Mature rock garden**
A well-planted mature rock garden with carefully chosen plants can offer as much colour and interest as any other part of the garden.

Scree plants

Plants with a slow rate of growth come mostly from the highest altitudes and high rocky places and these are also often of low hummock or cushion formation, with tiny leaves or rosettes. These are known as scree plants, needing very little soil, but very good drainage. They are found growing at altitudes of 30,000ft (9,144m), where they may be under snow for six months of the year. But they remain relatively dry over this long period, as little or no moisture soaks down to their roots until the snow begins to melt. Then, as summer comes, one can see the almost miraculous sight of flowers peering through the remaining snow. It is this short period of growth, with cold nights, that has made such plants so diminutive.

As might be expected, these high altitude alpines are the most difficult to adapt to garden conditions, as they need gritty soil but object to both winter wetness and summer drought and heat. They are often grown to good advantage in stone sinks and troughs; but some are best in what is known as an alpine house (see chapter 6 on page 63), where the glass covering keeps off winter wetness and where moisture requirements can be met as and when needed.

Because of their special needs, only a few scree plants are mentioned in the A–Z directory (starting on page 99), but the variety available is so wide that a number of cushion-forming plants, which are less fussy, are included.

↗ **Scree garden**
Slate chippings are used here as a soil topping, giving the impression that the planting looks like a scree slope.

↗ **Slate mulch**
Here, slate chippings are spread between plants on a flat surface, used purely as a decorative mulch.

ALPINE TIP

It is fun to choose plants for your rockery, rock garden, wall, containers or alpine house – but patience is one of the prime virtues of the good alpine gardener. A visit to a famous garden, flower show or even the garden centre will inspire you to recreate what you see and the temptation might be to rush out and do it. But don't. Consider all things carefully, otherwise you will waste time, effort and money. The fact that you are reading this book, of course, means that you are already on the right path!

Bushy alpines

Another habit group is those plants that have a semi-shrubby formation. This may be upright or more spreading, and evergreen or deciduous as far as foliage is concerned, but comes from a more-or-less central root, with life retained above ground over winter, regardless of whether foliage is lost. These are described as having a bushy or trailing habit and are generally easy to grow. Examples of the erect and bushy types are seen in *Iberis*, *Helianthemum*, *Gypsophila* and some of the trailing *Penstemon*.

In the wild, most bush-forming alpines are found on hills and mountains bordering the Mediterranean or in the Near and Middle East. In these areas, summers are hot and dry but, when roots are able to penetrate deeply into rock crevices and walls, plants can still survive. Unlike those growing in a mild, moist climate, leaves hold very little sap, which is often an indication of low rainfall and a short rainy season. It is in this short season that new growth and flowering takes place. This range of plants will often flourish in gardens, but they may need trimming to keep neat and shapely.

Clump-formers

Alpines may also be clump-forming, which means that they do not spread by underground shoots when they expand in size. The large genus of *Campanula* includes some with this habit. Those with the habit of spreading underground can be a nuisance, as they invade neighbouring plants. The A–Z directory mentions any specific species that are clump-formers and those plants with a rampant nature.

Mat-formers

Other groups of alpines have mat-like growth. These (together with carpeters) often root down into the soil as they spread with varying rapidity, and more often than not keep themselves

← **Mat-forming alpines**

Some alpines are mat-formers, such as this *Eriogonum kennedyi* var. *alpigenum*.

clothed over winter. Some smother themselves with flowers in summer, but others are grown purely for their silvery and green foliage. These are useful plants and are among the easiest to grow: they include such well-known subjects as *Aubrieta*, alpine phlox and thyme.

Herbaceous alpines

Some alpines die down in true herbaceous character to a live, but scarcely visible, rootstock during winter dormancy. They are often found in alpine meadows or anywhere with a fair depth of soil. Because of competition with other plants, including grasses, they survive by sharing their natural habitat. Some associate with plants that have a different root system, allowing roots to feed at different levels. Others grow at different heights and share air and light. As a result, some alpine plants grow better if they are in association with others.

↗ Herbaceous alpines
Some alpines are larger herbaceous subjects, such as this *Zauschneria californica* subsp. *garrettii*.

CLUMP-FORMING ALPINES

Some alpines are clump formers, such as this Saxifraga x megaseiflora 'Josef Kapek'. This particular specimen is being grown in a pot, staged on the bench of an alpine house, where its preferred conditions of growth can be precisely catered for.

CHAPTER

02

HOW TO USE ALPINES IN THE GARDEN

Good proportions

It is important to design a rockery feature with the right proportion of plants to rock; too many plants are confusing to the eye, too much rock and it can look like a building site.

WHERE TO GROW ALPINES

Although a rockery is the ideal environment for growing alpine plants, there are various other suitable situations in the garden. These can be loosely divided into the following: rockeries, raised beds, walls, cracks, crannies and paving, containers, tufa rock and the alpine greenhouse. Whichever you choose, you must always try to follow the rules on aspect.

Aspect

The vast majority of alpines prefer an open, sunny position, well drained but not too dry. The most difficult site for growing alpines, as with taller herbaceous or border plants, is dry shade under trees where the roots starve the soil and overhanging branches block sunlight and air. The 'perfect' situation of a sunny, open slope may not always be available but, as long as the soil drainage is good, other aspects may be used. However, the least favourable direction for a rock garden to face is eastwards, which is cold and unsympathetic. If you are restricted in the choice of site, then preparations should be made to give the plants the best possible chance and to choose which plants will adapt.

Some alpines, including forms of *Cassiope*, *Cyclamen*, *Gaultheria*, *Haberlea*, *Primula*, *Ramonda* and *Vaccinium* prefer a modicum of shade, or a cooler aspect pointing away from the sun (in the northern hemisphere this will be north-facing and in the southern hemisphere this will be south-facing).

← **Typical rock garden**

A rock garden is the traditional – and ideal – way to display alpine plants, but not all gardens have room for one.

Rockeries

With a flat or gently sloping garden with no natural rock formation, think carefully before introducing rocks. Some people may feel that alpines without rocks are incongruous, but this is purely a matter of personal choice. I believe that if you wish to grow alpines for their beauty, it is best to limit the use of rocks to easing slopes or to gently break up any tendency to flatness in the garden.

A clumsily or unskilfully constructed rockery or rock garden can spoil the overall design. It can also prove an expensive outlay, difficult to maintain and restrictive if the rocks take up too much space or are badly placed.

However, a properly constructed rockery can provide a great many cracks, crannies and crevices between the rocks, and these form ideal homes for plants such as *Sempervivum*,

Saxifraga, small *Dianthus*, *Saponaria* and *Sedum*. The creation of a small rockery and rock garden is discussed and shown on pages 42–45.

↑ Focal points
Large rocks can be used to create focal points in the rockery garden.

← Slate garden
Rock gardens that are made from slate can be very attractive, and look even better if combined with some running water.

Raised beds

If you wish to grow alpines without the use of rocks, it is worth considering making a raised bed dedicated to them, particularly as so many alpine species are tiny. Also, if bending down is difficult, a raised bed enables you to appreciate your plants at close quarters.

If there is no objection to stooping, an alternative is to have a 'walkabout bed'. This can be made using stone or bricks around the perimeter, which is filled in with a suitable soil mixture. It is then easy to arrange access across the bed with flat stones or bricks to tread on. Unless the ground has sufficient natural slope to form a terrace or bank, this will involve building a low wall.

↗ Raised beds
Raised alpine beds, seen here at the Royal Horticultural Society garden at Wisley, UK, enable the gardener to tend plants with less stooping.

↗ Walkabout beds
A 'walkabout bed', edged with brick, stone or tile, can be filled with appropriate plants to make an alpine feature.

Walls

Rustic walls are an excellent habitat for alpine plants. Many will thrive in the small spaces between the blocks or stones in a wall. It is, of course, easier to put in the plants as the wall is being built, but an old wall can usually be colonized, if not by actual plants, then by mixing the seeds of alpines with damp sand and dropping it into the crevices. Many of the seeds will fail to germinate, or they will start to grow and then succumb to dryness, the elements or pests, but usually enough will survive to begin colonization. This is a good way to achieve a natural looking alpine feature, as the plants will grow where they survive rather than where they have been placed.

ALPINE TIP

Walls can also be free-standing and two-sided, which means one side can be shady and the other sunny, or they can be built hollow with the centre filled with soil. This provides a number of aspects, as the sides, the ends and the top of the wall can all be used for a diversity of plants. These wall features can be extremely decorative and economical of space.

↗ Tufa rock wall
This tufa rock wall, photographed in winter, has a few hardy ferns growing in it; in the spring and summer it is covered in alpine flowers.

Cracks, crannies and paving

The cracks and crannies between paving stones offer just the conditions most alpines need. Their heads will be in the light while their roots will be in cool, moist soil beneath the paving stones, and these stones will protect their stems from wet soil. Alpines planted like this can also look good because they break up the hard lines of a man-made paved area.

This works less well in a low-lying, sunless paved area that is vulnerable to collecting large puddles after rainfall. But even here you may succeed with carefully selected and interesting ferns and mosses; for more detail on these, however, you should consult specialist books.

↗ Plants in crevices
These *Sempervivum* are very much 'at home' in the tiniest of crevices in rocks.

↓ Plants in paving
Plants set into areas of block paving will, in time, help to break up the hard structural lines.

CHAMOMILE IN PAVING
||||||||||||||||||||||||||||||||||||||||||||||||||||||||||||||||||||||||||||||

Established plants growing in paving can look most attractive; here chamomile is grown in block paving and when walked upon will produce a pleasing fragrance. Chamomile will not tolerate particularly heavy foot traffic, so you should only plant it where the occasional passer-by will walk.

ALPINE TIP
||||||||||||||||||||||||||||||||||||||||||||||||||||||||||||||||||||||||||||||

Suitable alpines for paved areas are usually low-growing mat- or small clump-formers, but do not be afraid to put in the occasional upright or small sub-shrub. These are semi-woody plants that are not particularly herbaceous or perennial in nature, yet survive for many years, such as heathers. Even one or two slow-growing or dwarf conifers can look good.

Containers

Growing alpines in containers is very popular, particularly among people with small gardens. Traditionally, old stone sinks and troughs were used as containers. This was first done by Clarence Elliott, an English alpine nurseryman of the last century who wanted to put some old sinks to good use and came up with the idea of creating little rock features in them.

Sinks look most at home standing on a patio or paved area near the house but the glaze used to make the sink look shiny needs to be coated before it can be used for growing alpines (see page 57). Garden centres also offer many containers made from materials such as stone and concrete, moulded resin, wood and plastic.

↗ Sink garden
Sink gardens are a traditional way to grow alpines, first inspired by the English nurseryman Clarence Elliott.

↓ Alpine containers
Containers of all shapes and sizes can be used for alpines.

Tufa rock

Tufa is a decorative, porous limestone rock that is often used in alpine beds and on rock gardens. It is formed when lime is deposited in a stream, building up over the years around debris such as small twigs and leaves. With age, the outer surface of the rock hardens while the inside remains soft enough for plant roots to penetrate and extract all the nutrients required to sustain them. The rock is porous so it will hold a reservoir of water. Although a limestone, tufa is a form called magnesium lime which does not lock up the iron, enabling lime-haters to be grown in it, side-by-side with lime-lovers. High alpine cushion plants, which have low nutrient and low water requirements are the most suitable.

A chunk of tufa can be drilled and hollowed to create a container-like structure that can be filled with a gritty, free-draining compost. Or small pieces of tufa can be chipped off a larger piece, and used to create decorative, miniature mountain scapes, so enhancing sinks, troughs and other containers.

But for me, the best use of tufa is purely as a planted chunk! A lump of it can be drilled and hollowed easily in designated places, then planted up with a range of plants. As the plants become established, their roots penetrate the porous rock and they grow into characteristically hard and compact specimens. A large piece of tufa can be home to 20 or more plants and can become a feature of great beauty and interest. For more detail see pages 52–3.

→ **Tufa rock feature**
This large piece of tufa rock has been planted up with alpines to make an attractive rock-like feature.

The alpine greenhouse

As a student at the world-famous garden at Wisley in Surrey, UK, my favourite place to be was the alpine house. This was a purpose-built greenhouse with a low 'pitch', to bring the plants as near as possible to the glass. Also, it had continuous ventilation along both sides of the roof and at the sides at staging level.

However, an ordinary greenhouse can be adapted and work just as well. Additional vents can usually be installed at little extra cost. The steeper 'pitch' of a traditional greenhouse is not a particularly serious drawback. For best transmission of sunlight, it should ideally be placed with an east-west run; however, if by necessity a house has to run north-south, make sure the door (if only at one end) is at the end that faces the sun.

There are two schools of thought as to whether alpine houses should be heated or not. Some gardeners like to be able to exclude frost, while others prefer to have no form of heating at all. There is only a marginal difference in the types of plants you can grow, and bearing in mind the price of fuels and energy, it probably is not worth going to the extreme of warming a house in this way.

What is more relevant, however, is that the structure given over to growing alpines should not also be used for growing other types of plant. The differences in growing conditions are likely to be very different, and you may end up failing with one type or the other, or both. More details on keeping an alpine house are provided in Chapter 6.

↗ **Purpose-built greenhouse**
Enthusiasts can grow alpines in a greenhouse especially designed for them; there needs to be plenty of ventilation to keep air circulating around the plants.

↓ **Bed in an alpine house**
The best alpine houses have benches where pots of alpine plants, when in season, can be displayed in full view by sinking them into deep sand beds.

CHAPTER

03

BUYING ALPINE PLANTS

Quality not quantity

The skill in building an alpine collection is in finding the plant you want, of the quality you want. To find both of these you will probably need to go to a specialist nursery. This plant is *Dodecatheon meadia* AGM.

SOURCES OF PLANTS

There are various ways of acquiring alpine plants. You can buy them, of course, or you can increase your stock of plants by propagating them from seed or cuttings.

Sadly, however, some people seem to consider theft as an acceptable way to obtain plants. Many alpine enthusiasts have had plants – sometimes rare and unusual ones – stolen from their alpine house or garden. Some form of garden security, from sensor lighting, locked gates at night, or even the use of alarms, may be entirely justified, particularly if your collection becomes valuable.

In my experience if you want something badly enough, all you have to do is ask and the chances are that the gardener in question will offer you a piece, especially as this can act as an insurance in case their own dies.

Specialist nurseries

Specialist nurseries are the best source of any plants that are collected as a hobby, as they can offer plenty of choice as well as quality (usually) and expertise. Specialist nurseries sell plants in various ways.

Visit the nursery: Obviously a personal visit to the nursery enables you to see the plants you are about to purchase but, more than this, it allows you to talk to the nursery staff who enjoy talking about their plants, and it is in their interest to encourage you to try new plants and to get the best out of your hobby.

Note also that for reasons of safety and public liability, not all specialist nurseries are open to members of the public, but just because they are not, does not mean that they necessarily have anything to hide, nor that their plants are in any way less worthy.

Mail order: Most of the best specialist nurseries will provide a catalogue of their stock so you can order plants by post. These are always worth

↗ Small conifers for sale
Buying alpines and associated rockery plants – small conifers, shrubs and bulbs – needs to be done with care and consideration, or you could end up with plants that are completely unsuitable.

↗ Specialist nurseries
Going to a nursery that specializes in alpine plants is a good idea, as you will be able to choose from a greater selection of plants.

getting hold of as they not only tell you what is available, but they often give cultural and descriptive information as well. These catalogues may incur a small charge, but are worth buying.

The more modern mail-order equivalent of choosing plants from a catalogue is the internet. Increasingly nurseries have their own websites and online catalogues, which, of course, are entirely free to view. Either way, remember that there will usually be an additional charge for postage and packing.

When buying plants via mail order you obviously do not see the plants before they arrive, but most reputable nurseries can be trusted to send out good plants. Stock can also run out, especially with a group of plants like alpines, as propagation and 'bulking up' of new stock can be a slow process. For this reason some nurseries ask that you list alternatives if the specific plants you need are not available.

Plants are normally only dispatched during the spring and autumn – the traditional times for planting and potting.

Garden centres

Alpines can usually be bought from garden centres, but the range of species and varieties offered is severely limited, and in many cases the treatment and quality of the plants usually leaves much to be desired. General garden centres are, however, useful for new entrants to the hobby of growing alpines, as plants are often less expensive, and the selection being offered is usually the more popular and frequently the easier-to-grow types.

ALPINE TIP

Don't forget: if you are going away on holiday, even for just a few days, make sure you have a back-up plan for receipt of plants you have ordered, such as a neighbour who can look after them until you return. If plants are left in a parcel for a long time you may be met with the sight of a rotting mass when it is eventually opened.

↗ **Mail order plants**
When plants bought by mail order arrive, they should be unpacked and watered immediately.

↗ **Alpines for beginners**
If you are a beginner at growing alpines, start with some of the easier-to-grow types, such as forms of alpine primula (*Primula allionii*). This is the cultivar 'Elizabeth Earle'.

RULES FOR CHOOSING PLANTS

Difficult and rare plants

If you are a beginner, it is not advisable to try to grow the more difficult or less common alpines; there is a high probability that they will perish under your care, which will be a waste of money, effort – and plants! Many of the easier-to-grow plants are also some of the most attractive – just because a plant may be rare does not mean that it will be especially beautiful.

The best advice is to start with the most commonly available species and varieties, as these will give you plenty of valuable experience in growing and caring for these plants, enabling you to be able to confidently progress to the more challenging types in time.

Pot-bound plants

The first thing to remember is that you should always choose a plant that looks healthy. Avoid any plant that has stunted growth or obvious signs of pests such as aphids. On the other hand do not go for the largest plants as these can be the most difficult to establish; a good, medium-sized plant, or even a small plant as long as it is not weedy, is what is required.

If roots are emerging from the bottom of the pot check that the plant is not too root-bound. Many that have a solid cylinder of roots will be difficult to establish.

↗ **Checking roots**
Check the roots of potted alpines before you buy them. This plant is on the verge of being pot-bound.

↗ **Dry plant**
If a potted alpine plant appears to be dry, then it has not been looked after very well at the nursery or garden centre, and there may be other things wrong with it as well.

CHECKING FOR COLOUR

If the alpine plant you are interested in buying already has a flower or two open, at least you are guaranteed of its colour when you get it home.

Flowering plants

There are some plants that are best seen in flower before being purchased. These are plants that have different colour forms or different flower shapes, some much better than others. For example, there are quite a large number of different *Geranium* species that have a range of petal shapes and colours. Obviously some will be more appealing to you than others. Plants raised at the nursery from seed are especially prone to variability, so these should be treated with caution – until you have seen them in flower. There are some specialist alpine nurseries whose custom depends on reliability and integrity, so these can usually be trusted to sell plants that are correctly named and labelled. Others are just keen to sell plant stock with little interest in accuracy, so be careful. You will soon get to know which plants are variable and which nurseries to go to for accuracy.

Another possible pitfall is the season in which you buy your plants. During the dormant season (usually the winter, or often other times of the year in the case of bulbous plants) you will have to buy plants on trust. During the growing season you will at least be able to see that there is a plant growing in the pot; if it is in flower you may even be able to identify it correctly as the exact species or variety you are seeking.

Established plants

Treat with caution any plants that have obvious signs of having just been dug up and hurriedly rammed into the pot. Some of these may make good plants, but others may have little or no roots or, even worse, broken stems. The most seriously traumatized plants may never recover from this treatment.

Perhaps the exception to this are forms of *Eranthis* (winter aconite) and *Galanthus* (snowdrop), which are best planted 'in the green' (that is, while they are still in leaf). It is acceptable – indeed preferable – to purchase them after they have been recently dug up.

AT HOME

When you get your alpines home, or on receipt of mail-ordered plants, unpack them immediately. Water them if necessary and stand them in a cool, shady place for a few days to acclimatize. Sometimes – but rarely these days – alpine plants will be sent out without a pot. Their roots will be wrapped in polythene with a little compost around them to keep them moist. The plants will require putting straight into a pot, even if they are destined eventually for planting on a rockery in the open garden.

Once the plants have been allowed to settle for a short while (perhaps for as little as a few days to a month or so) they should be transferred to their final position. This could be either to the open garden, a frame or an alpine house. But do not be in too much of a rush to plant outside; you should first make certain that your plants are big enough and sturdy enough.

ALPINE TIP

Sometimes you will be able to buy plants, particularly some of the woodland plants with thick, fleshy roots that have outgrown their pots. When you get them home you will be able to remove them from their pots and divide them into many smaller plants. If planted immediately and watered the vast majority should survive, so your one plant could turn into 5, 10, 20 or more. Experience will tell you what can be purchased in this state but, as a rule, avoid anything that is too pot-bound, especially if you are buying trees or shrubs.

↗ **Snowdrops 'in the green'**
Snowdrops (*Galanthus* spp) can be bought or transplanted, while 'in the green', in other words, while the leaves are still visible and before they have faded and dried to nothing.

04

CREATING A ROCK GARDEN

Alpine paving

Rock can be used in ways other than purely on a rock garden; here it has been used as the base and edging of an alpine walkway.

↘

BUILDING A ROCKERY

Constructing a rock garden can be laborious if you do it yourself, but expensive if you employ an expert to build the feature for you. Costs can be reduced by using local stone if it is available – it is likely to be cheaper than stone that has been imported to the area and will also look more natural. The cost of transporting heavy rocks a long distance can easily cost more than the material itself.

Whether you bring in the services of a landscaper, or you treat the project as a 'do-it-yourself' task, creating a rock feature can be incredibly satisfying.

Amount of rock needed: This will usually depend upon the building type adopted. For example, a site measuring, say, 150 sq ft (14m²) – which may sound big but is only approximate to an area roughly 12ft (10.5m) across and deep – can be made into a hugely worthwhile rock garden by using between 2–3 tons/tonnes of stone in various sizes and weights.

Transporting the rock: However small your rockery feature is, it will always be enhanced if you use reasonably large rocks – as large as can be comfortably handled. Lumps weighing as little as 10lb (4.5kg) can generally be carried without too much effort, whereas heavier pieces – say up to 200lb (90kg) – can be transported by using a sack truck running on planks.

Other ways to move stone include rolling it into position either on the ground or on boards, levering it using stout poles and sliding it by allowing it to sit on rollers (created by fashioning a few cylindrical wooden shafts, rather like thick broom handles). If you are inventive, quite large and heavy rocks can be moved with only reasonable effort. Rocks larger than 200lb (90kg) should really be lifted into place by mechanical diggers, fork-lift trucks or lorry hoists, but you are likely to need these services to be bought-in rather than to 'do-it-yourself'.

↖ **Sandstone rockery**
Building a rock garden, especially an intricate one with complex stone arrangements and running water, can be laborious and costly – but they do not always need to be as ambitious as this.

← **Rock choice**
Choose the rock carefully. To be in keeping with your immediate environment it should be local stone; besides, the further rock has to travel the more expensive it becomes.

↗ **Compost bin**
Home-made compost and leafmould are useful additions to the
soil that forms the core material of a rock garden.

← **Alpine paving**
Rock can be used in ways other than purely on a rock garden; here
it has been used as the base and edging of an alpine walkway.

The soil

Soil will probably be required to fill the spaces
behind the rocks as the rockery is constructed
and, as an approximate guide, 1 cu yd (0.75m³)
will be needed for each ton/tonne of rock. This
soil should be mixed with compost and ready for
use when building commences.

For the majority of alpines, no complicated
soil mixture is required. A good standard soil
can be prepared by mixing two parts of loam
(or good top-spit garden soil), one part of sharp
sand or fine grit, and one part of peat or peat-
substitute (such as coir fibre, composted bark
or leaf-mould). All parts are by volume rather
than weight. Before mixing these together,
add a generous sprinkling of bonemeal fertilizer.
No other feeding will be needed.

These mixes will answer the needs of the majority
of alpine plants. For any special plants, separate
composts can be mixed for individual 'pockets'.
High alpines, for example, prefer a more gritty
compost, so grit or sharp sand can be added in
greater quantity.

Alpine plants fall into two major categories:
those plants which must have neutral or acid
soil, and those which like, or will tolerate, lime.
The lime-haters are very particular in their
requirements, but most of the lime-lovers will
tolerate lime-free conditions. For example, nearly
all types of *Aubrieta* and *Dianthus* are lime-lovers,
but will thrive well enough without it. On the
other hand, most members of the heather and
Rhododendron family, and all the Asiatic autumn-
flowering gentians, will not thrive in alkaline soils.

Drainage

Alpine plants will suffer in ground that is sodden, which is why the soil needs to contain a medium to high proportion of sharp sand or grit. Yes, the plants like plenty of water, particularly in summer, but this water must pass rapidly through the soil and not develop into a bog around the plants' roots.

If your garden soil is clay, and especially if the site is level, it will be necessary to dig a few deep sump holes and to fill them with some form of rough drainage, such as broken stone, brick or large-grade gravel, so that surplus moisture can soak away and not collect around the roots of the plants. On a sloping site, provide drainage by digging a few channels downhill, and fill these with similar materials.

Weeds

Before you start to put rocks down, the site must be thoroughly cleared of debris, especially perennial weeds. These may have to be dug out, which itself can be an arduous job, but even the smallest piece left in the ground of, for example, bindweed (*Convolvulus* spp) will grow up through the rock garden and cause a great deal of trouble.

Construction

When you come to building the rockery, keep the site clear of materials or there will be a constant need to move things. It is a good idea to arrange the stone you are using in an arc or a circle around the site, with the best face pointing inwards. In this way you will be able to see it all instantly and there is no need to be searching constantly through a pile of stone for the right piece. The least number of times the stone is moved the better, especially for you!

The whole structure should be a mixture of soil and stones, but don't make a heap of earth and dot the stones around on it. Any stone placed on top of loose earth will in time sink into it and

the overall shape will be lost. The core of the structure must consist of both stone and soil. There is no reason why this stone should be the same as that on the surface; it can be larger lumps of rubble or even concrete. This core will help support the heavier rocks on the surface, as well as providing the plants with cool root runs.

In the following pages I will explain how to build a simple rockery bank. A more complex version of this, even a large stand-alone rockery garden, needs to follow the same construction principles.

↗ **Weeding**
It is crucial that all perennial weeds are removed from rock-garden soil prior to the laying of rocks or setting out of plants.

↗ **Gravel**
Gravel is available is varying grades and sizes. The small grades are appropriate for mixing in soil, the large grades for piling into drainage sumps, and the medium grades for mulching and finishing off a rock garden.

↗ **Rockery steps**

Steps on a rock garden should be flat, firm, stable and as wide as you can make them. The wider the steps, the more convenient they are to use, and the larger the rock garden appears.

↘

LEVELS AND STEPS

A large, highly sloping rock garden may require, or be enhanced by, a series of steps or a sloping path up which one can walk in order to see things at close quarters, or to look at a view. Sloping paths can be awkward and dangerous in wet or icy weather, so I would always, where appropriate, choose steps.

ALPINE TIP

If possible, and you can plan ahead sufficiently, the site should be cleared at least six months before construction begins so that any remaining weeds can be identified. There will of course be annual and perennial weed seeds left in the soil, but these should not germinate and become weeds as they will be covered deeply by soil and rock.

BUILDING A SIMPLE ROCKERY BANK

1. Make sure the base is firm, by tamping it down with a thick wooden pole. Then lay out the first layer of stones, which should be half buried below the normal soil surface. Make sure that the rock is sloping slightly back towards the centre of the structure. The reason for this is so that the rain will run back into the centre of the rock garden. If it slopes the other way there will be areas that could be permanently dry; at the same time the water falling over the front of the rock could erode away the soil underneath it.

2. Chip the stone as required. Do not use stone that is the wrong shape, so that it protrudes from the rest of the stone layer; if it does, it will look unnatural and unappealing. If there are visible strata lines on the stone make certain that they all run the same way.

3. Lay the second course of rock. You can stagger them like bricks in a wall, or you can stack them as seen here. This stacking may look unnatural, but then if you think about it, so will the staggered look. The aim is to create a rockery that has its hard lines and joins covered over by natural-looking plants, so it won't make much difference where the joins are. The rocks should blend together either in outcrops or continuous building. Do not lay them in isolated splendour or put them on their smallest ends so that they stand up like pinnacles.

4. Bury every rock used so that its base cannot be seen. After every course of rock is laid, backfill with the soil so that each rock is properly bedded into position.

5. If there is space, a second bank of rock can be started at a position slightly forward or behind the first-laid bank. This offers greater gardening potential, giving the whole feature a secondary element and adding much more interest.

6. The final task at this stage should be to tidy up the front area. Make the walkway immediately in front of the rock a flat and stable place to stand, from where you can observe the feature at close quarters.

PLANTING A SIMPLE ROCKERY BANK

1. Start planting your rockery feature by siting the larger subjects such as any dwarf conifers or other shrubs. Still in their containers, stand them on the rockery so that you are happy with their position. Also, twist them around as plants usually have a 'front' and 'back', where the former is better balanced, with leaves and/or flowers seeming to be facing outwards.

2. When you are happy with the way the plant will look once planted, set it to one side and dig a hole. For larger plants you will need a space to do this. Take out a hole that is wider and deeper than the rootball of the plant. Place a little well-rotted organic matter (such as garden compost or leafmould, or even animal manure, but this should only be used with large, woody plants) in the bottom of the hole, mixing it with the soil there.

3. Remove the pot and gently place the plant's rootball into the hole. If the roots are particularly matted and congested – indicating that the plant was in its pot for too long – you can gently tease some of them out so they are hanging loose of the rootball. This will help the plant to establish in its new home.

4. Check that the top of the rootball is not sitting proud of the surrounding soil surface, nor that it is sunken beneath it. Then, with the spade, backfill with the prepared soil mixture described earlier. Firm around the roots as you go; do not be afraid to 'stick the boot in', as you can usually firm the soil more effectively this way – but always make sure you do not cause damage to the rootball itself. Water the plant to settle it in.

5. Once the bigger plants have been installed, you can attend to the smaller alpines. These should be planted with a trowel, and in each case a hole should be made, the plant put into position and then firmed and watered. With small alpines you do not need to incorporate organic matter – and you should not use your foot to firm them in either as you are much more likely to trample them.

6. Finally, where there are gaps between the larger shrubs/conifers and the small alpine plants, or at the front of a rockery bank, it is a good idea to plant small bulbs. Snowdrops, *Crocus*, *Muscari* and *Iris reticulata* all make good rockery bulbs, and light up a spring garden.

FINISHING OFF A SIMPLE ROCKERY BANK

1. The most appropriate way to finish off a rock garden, although it is not compulsory, is to lay a layer of small-grade gravel, grit or chippings all over the exposed soil. The layer needs to be just ½ –1in (1–2.5cm) deep. Its purpose is to conserve moisture, make weeds easier to pull out, and to prevent mud splash on the small, delicate alpine leaves and flowers. For some reason, also, finishing off a rock garden in this way looks entirely in keeping.

2. Once you have sprinkled the gravel or chippings by hand or by shovel, they need to be raked level. This will only be possible, of course, if there is enough space for the rake to be manoeuvred in between the rocks, otherwise smooth out the gravel by hand.

CAVES AND GROTTOS

Some of the world's largest and best rock gardens contain caves and grottos, which are mainly artificial rather than naturally occurring. As long as you have the space and money to have one constructed, there is no reason why you should not have one in your own rock garden. The one pictured here could be almost any size, and is not especially difficult to construct, although some of the rocks would be very heavy.

Ideally a cave or grotto should be set into a natural bank. If the bank is not very high, the whole feature could be sunk into the ground a little way to give the cave entrance more height. If there is no bank available, it could all be constructed against an old brick wall as long as rocks continue on either side to make it look more convincing.

Good-sized, block-like pieces of rock are easier to build with than lots of small, roundish pieces. The cave has to be built up rather like a house, so the more square the rock, the better.

The entrance to the cave will need a lintel stone. This must be strong and wide enough to span the entrance comfortably. It will almost certainly be one of the heaviest stones and should be hand-picked from the supplier's yard or quarry. Also, the cave must have a good foundation to ensure that the whole structure does not subside or crack. It will, after all, be extremely heavy.

We will not go into the intricacies of the construction now, for this is likely to be beyond the do-it-yourself capabilities of most people. As an idea, and a conceptual feature of a rockery garden, however, it could be worth considering.

↑ **Fern grotto**

This grotto would suit a large rockery feature, but even a small rock garden can accommodate a small cave or grotto.

INCORPORATING WATER

Pond styles

Rock gardens and water features often go hand-in-hand. A small water feature could be a pebble fountain or a free-standing half-barrel with a pretty trickling urn, both of which are ideal accompaniments to a tiny town garden or patio area. Larger waterfalls and cascades tumbling over well-placed rock, into a large, lower-level pond are what many of us aspire to.

Garden ponds, perhaps 3–6ft (1–2m) across, are what most gardeners can realistically create, and these can be wonderful and rewarding to observe and nurture.

Formal: Formal ponds are particularly suitable where space is limited. They are either circular, oval or have straight lines, such as a square, rectangle or some other geometric shape. They tend to look best in more formal surroundings, such as near the house, or in conjunction with other features such as straight paths and patios. They can also be raised or sunken, which can add another attractive dimension to the garden.

For most of us, the perfect pond is one in which there is some form of moving water. It may be the trickle of a little fountain, or a big gusher with a larger water feature. Formal ponds lend themselves to waterfalls, but not so much to natural-looking rockery cascades which, by their nature, are informal.

Informal: Informal ponds are irregular in shape – and look the best for most rockery gardens. Informal ponds may have soft, sweeping curves with few, if any, straight lines or sharp angles. This type of design looks at its best in a garden planted in a relaxed way – a sort of cottage garden, with flowers of all sizes and colours.

↗ Tumbling water feature
Running water on a rockery feature need not interfere with the alpine plants growing in adjacent positions, as long as the water course has been constructed well.

↗ Waterfall
A waterfall is so-called when there is a clear drop; when water tumbles over rocks it is referred to as a 'cascade'.

Still water: A still-water pond is the most basic type of pond, with no 'sophisticated' appeal, such as a fountain or waterfall, and no 'mechanical filtration' using pumps. This may sound rather boring, yet in many cases is better if you wish to keep fish and grow many types of aquatic plant – especially waterlilies, which hate too much moving water around their stems and leaves.

Fish or 'mixed' ponds: 'Fish pond' is the accepted phrase, but perhaps 'mixed pond' would be better, for although a selection of fish may be kept in it, there would undoubtedly be plants and pondweed, insect life and very probably amphibious life such as toads, frogs and newts.

Fish can be kept either in the lower pool at the base of a waterfall or cascade, or in a still water pool set within the rock garden.

The only fixed rules about keeping fish in an outdoor pond are that the types of fish kept should be fully hardy and not 'tender exotics' which would come to harm during a cold winter. The quantity and size of the fish you introduce depends on the dimensions of the pond, or more accurately, the volume of water held in the pond.

↗ **Bubble fountain**

Fountains can have a place in the pool of a large rock garden, but it is better if it is kept low (such as this bubble fountain) to avoid spray falling on nearby plants.

Fountains and waterfalls

Water that is 'moving' – spurting, trickling, cascading and even plummeting – is one of the joys of pond-keeping. Smaller features may include spurting frogs, millstones, lion's heads and even peeing urchins. Then there are the larger features requiring the movement of a greater water volume, such as streams, waterfalls, long cascades and high-rise fountains.

Waterfalls: These can be made to spill gently over a shallow sill, or gush in torrents over a high ledge. If the water is merely tipping and tumbling over rocks, it is called a 'cascade'.

There are prefabricated, moulded units available to act as the 'header' to a waterfall, and they are simple to install. All you need to worry about is that they are level from side to side, and that the lip protrudes sufficiently over the pond, and at a suitable height, to enable a body of water to fall into the pond rather than onto surrounding ground. The hosepipe, linking the pump to the header pool, should be carefully hidden.

Cascades: Most cascades are modelled along natural lines, but modern and contemporary equivalents, using sheets of glass, stainless steel and wooden channels, are becoming more popular.

A domestic garden cascade can be fairly vertical, with a series of rocks protruding from each other forming the water course, or a shallow, nearly level course, where the water will appear more as a stream.

Prefabricated sections are available from most large garden centres. They can be bought as a short, self-contained header pool/cascade, or as several units that fit together to make longer courses.

Water feature materials

Ponds need to be watertight and, within reason, it does not really matter how this is achieved. When it comes to the material used to form the base and sides of a pond there are three main options:preformed rigid glass fibre or plastic liners, flexible polythene, PVC and butyl liners and concrete. The following three areas will need to be considered before you make your choice.

Cost: The price of liner for a pond of a given size is very similar, whether you opt for the pre-formed type or flexible sheeting, but the cost of liners will vary according to where you buy them. For example, a liner bought from a high-quality garden centre will, almost certainly, cost more than if bought from a town market, or by a mail-order supplier. Both flexible and pre-formed pond liners come in various grades of thickness, and this also complicates any price comparison. In reality, after all variables have been taken into account, there is little difference in cost between the two types of liner.

Ease of installation: In its simplest form, making a pond with a flexible liner involves digging a hole, placing the liner into it and filling it with water. However, without paying attention to trimming, folding, tucking and, possibly, glueing, the end result may be less than satisfactory.

On the other hand, a pre-formed pond is ready to be sunk into a hole in its chosen place. The hole needs to be dug to exactly the right shape and size and kept perfectly level, however, and this is easier said than done.

Both types of liner need underlay or soft backing to prevent large stones from penetrating the material once the pond has been filled with water. Indeed, the quality of the soil, and the ease with which you can create a hole in it, may be the single determining factor.

↗ Pond liners
Pre-formed pond liners made from plastic, PVC or glass-fibre are available in various shapes and styles.

Ease of maintenance: Ponds made of concrete do tend to be the most labour-intensive in terms of on-going maintenance. Ground movement can create cracks and old concrete can become brittle. Repairing kits and sealants are expensive.

Cheap-grade flexible liners, when exposed to sunlight, will degrade in time. Liners with a guarantee of 10 years or more should be sought (even better are those with a 35-year guarantee). Preformed glass fibre or moulded plastic ponds are extremely rigid, and usually thick enough to repel knocks and grazes. However, a badly placed boulder that is set underneath the filled pond can potentially do more damage to a pre-formed liner than to a flexible one.

PEAT BEDS

It is generally thought that alpine plants come from high mountain places where the plants are half-starved most of the time. The idea of a rock garden comprising peat blocks and acid soil would probably never come into most gardeners' minds.

The peat bed is, however, ideal for certain types of alpine plants, especially those that grow further down the mountain, in woodland or open moist conditions. Putting this into the garden dramatically increases the number of plants you can grow and can be well worth considering.

In the past, peat has been the unquestioned main material, with peat blocks playing the part of the 'rock', in holding a bank of peaty soil in place. Peat blocks were easily available and affordable. However, quite a few gardeners these days choose not to use them, because of dwindling natural peat reserves and the ensuing loss of many wildlife habitats as a result of peat extraction. Instead, gardeners prefer to use leafmould as the basis of their compost, supported in place by wooden or log edging.

There is a wide range of plants that will cheerfully grow in these beds. In the walls themselves you can plant ramondas and primulas, and even shrubby plants, such as vacciniums, which are useful in binding the wall with their roots. In the soil behind the block or edging, any acid-loving plant is possible, but with subjects such as *Epimedium*, which has a spreading tendency, make certain that they are planted far enough apart so as not to swamp each other after the first year.

← Peat block garden

Peat blocks were the traditional material for building the sides and edges of a peat bed, but they are difficult to come by these days, and in any case wooden edging is more sustainable.

↘

A 'TUFA GARDEN'

As we saw on page 26, tufa is a decorative, porous limestone rock and is often used to create alpine features. A large chunk of tufa can be drilled in places, using a power drill with a large masonry bit, or you can use a hammer and chisel. Whichever method you employ, the aim is to create small, container-like depressions.

Putting an established plant into tufa can be a bit of a problem. If the roots of the plant are small enough then it can be gently inserted into the drilled hole, and gritty compost added, packed around the roots and pressed to hold in place. Then the plant should be watered in using a watering can fitted with a fine rose end, to avoid

a large spurt of water washing all of the compost out. However, if the plant is a little on the large side for the size of hole, you may prefer to take the alpine plant out of its pot and wash all the soil off the roots. Then wrap the roots in damp paper tissue. This 'tube' of roots can then be eased into the hole and the gap between it and the sides of the hole gently filled with gritty, free-draining compost. The roots will soon grow away through the tissue and into the compost.

If you place a large piece of tufa directly onto a rockery, it can look a little incongruous, as the main stone (sandstone, granite or even limestone) would look entirely different. It is usually better therefore to display a 'tufa garden' on a hard-standing area such as a patio, or raised slightly on a raised bed. It should also be sited in a position of part-shade.

↗ **Chiselling tufa**
Holes can be drilled into a large piece of tufa, or you can use a hammer and chisel.

↗ **Small alpines**
Only small alpine plants should be used when planting tufa rock, as it can be difficult to work the roots into the prepared holes.

ALPINE TIP

If, having experienced the delights of tufa – which is a very lightweight material – you would like to use it elsewhere in the garden, there is no reason why you cannot excavate an area to a depth of, say 12–18in (30–45cm), and fill it with alpine compost. Placing one or two medium-sized chunks of tufa so that they are seemingly coming out of the ground, sporting a variety of alpine plants, can look most fetching.

← **Tufa rockery**
A tufa rockery feature can sit on a patio, be raised on a stand, or be placed in a convenient part of the garden – but it can sometimes look incongruous when placed on or just next to a rock garden, as the two styles of rock are likely to be very different.

↗ **Planting up tufa**
Use a very gritty compost to fill between the plant's roots and the sides of the holes.

05

ALPINES IN CONTAINERS

Contained splendour

Alpines are the perfect choice for garden containers as they tend to prefer drier conditions and less feeding than most garden plants. They are also small enough not to need re-potting every few months.

SINKS AND TROUGHS

One of the joys of alpine gardening is that it can be carried out on any scale. You can construct a rock garden covering several acres or restrict yourself to a plot no more than 12in² (30cm²). Even in such a small area as this it is possible to grow quite a number of plants.

Sinks and troughs are perfect for growing alpines in containers and they are particularly suitable for small gardens. Their advantages are twofold. First, the containers are small enough for you to control the growing conditions, such as the composition of the soil and the degree of drainage. They are easy to water and, if necessary, can easily be covered in times of excessive rain or extreme cold. Thus the sink makes an ideal home for plants that need that extra bit of attention and many difficult-to-grow plants have been successfully grown there.

Secondly, they are small enough to be used in the smallest of gardens, even on a balcony if that is the only space available. This small size also makes them ideal for the elderly and disabled as they are easy to tend and yet give the pleasure of creating a landscaped garden in miniature and growing quite a number of plants.

Natural stone

When sink gardens first became popular in the 1920s and 1930s, the sinks being used were made from stone and slate. They were being 'recycled' after a lifetime of use as water and feeding troughs for animals and even troughs for catching the blood of slaughtered animals in abattoirs. Such troughs were being replaced by cheaper and easier-to-maintain materials such as galvanized metals and glazed ceramics.

The rough stone containers made ideal settings for the alpine plants, and many alpine experts would say that these materials have never been bettered. Being old they had mellowed and had acquired a patina of age, much like the rocks of the alpines' native habitats.

Unfortunately, the supply of such sinks has dried up. The limited supply has either been snapped up for the purpose, or been discarded or destroyed unwittingly by their owners. Rarely

↘ Patio alpine container

A low container sporting a range of colourful alpine plants can become a feature of a terrace or patio.

↘ Alpine trough

Troughs such as this have become a traditional way to display a range of alpines outdoors. Note how trailing plants at the front help to break up the hard lines of the container.

the odd one or two may be found, tucked away in an odd corner of a farm, but the most likely source is on the second-hand market where they can command quite high prices.

Sinks (whether of natural stone or man-made – see below) are ready to use as soon as they are acquired, as they already have a drainage hole in them – the plug-hole. Troughs on the other hand were designed to hold water permanently and therefore have no hole in the bottom. Buying a second-hand trough that has already been used for the purpose of growing alpines is likely to have had drainage holes drilled in to it, but if it hasn't, you will need to do this before creating your own alpine garden in it.

Covering glazed sinks

Alpine sinks and troughs fashioned from old glazed sinks – and sometimes ceramic or metal troughs – have become the modern alternative to natural stone and slate, and they are economically viable, more widely available and hugely attractive when built properly. The white glazed sinks that replaced stone ones in so many cottages have themselves now been superseded by stainless steel and other modern materials.

Most are deep and a good shape in which to grow alpines, but their exterior appearance leaves much to be desired. Fortunately, a technique was developed in the mid-1900s which involves coating the outside of the sink with a cement mixture called 'hypertufa' which, while not looking exactly rock-like, softens the colour and outline of the sink, so making a good setting for alpines.

Prepare the glazed sink by thoroughly washing it to remove any dirt or grease. Ideally, then place the sink in its final resting position, as it will be extremely heavy once coated, and even more so when filled up with soil. The final resting place of the sink should not be on the ground, but propped up on bricks – this way you

can coat some or all of the underside, and you will also be able to grip onto the sink better if you need to move it later on.

Mix together equal parts by volume of sand, cement and peat (or peat alternative such as coir). Peat or coir helps with the ageing process, producing a rock-like patina. In a bucket, add the three ingredients followed by enough water until it reaches a thick, creamy consistency. Then cover it over with a damp cloth to prevent rapid drying out. Then cover completely the outside of the sink with a layer of adhesive, such as Unibond. Continue this layer over the rim and down some 3in (8cm) on the inside. Apply the hypertufa mixture directly on to the adhesive, making certain that it is firmly stuck.

When the sink is covered, protect it with a damp cloth so that the hypertufa does not dry out too quickly, which can cause cracking. When partly dry, you can fashion the covering by brushing, which gives a sandy-finish, or scoring with wire brush or knife, to make it look more natural – but do not overdo this as too much will spoil the appearance.

↘ **Hypertufa-covered sink**
This alpine sink could be improved: the hypertufa covering over the white glaze has worn or fallen away, and needs re-applying.

↘

OTHER CONTAINERS

Hypertufa containers

You can also use the hypertufa mixture to make a whole container. The advantage of this is that you can tailor it to the size that best suits the position in which you want to put it.

The simplest way to do this is to use two cardboard boxes, where one can fit inside the other with about a 2in (5cm) gap all around. Sit the larger box on the ground, and support

its sides by standing bricks on the outside, but butting against the sides – this will stop the sides sagging when filled with cement.

Place a 2in (5cm) layer of hypertufa in the base of the larger box; it is a good idea while you are doing this also to place one or two small blocks of wood in the base. When the finished item is dried, these pieces of wood can then be removed to leave holes for drainage.

Place the smaller box on the top of this layer, centrally placed within the larger box. Fill the gap between the two boxes with more of the mixture. Place more bricks in the inner box

↗ **Drilling drainage holes**
This small container has been created from hypertufa, set in a mould. If there is no drainage hole present, one would need to be drilled.

↗ **Crocks**
Crocks are needed in the base of the container to assist the outflow of surplus moisture.

↗ **Gravel covering**
Gravel or chippings are applied to the surface of the compost after planting.

↗ **Completed container**
The completed hypertufa container needs to be set on a stable, flat surface.

to support its sides, or fill it with soil, sand or gravel. Tamp the hypertufa down in the gap, to ensure that there are no air pockets. When finished, cover it with a damp cloth and leave for a couple of days to dry.

Shop-bought containers

There is a wide range of containers available, made from, plastic, terracotta, reconstituted stone, wood and moulded resin. The plastic ones are the cheapest but some are rather garish so look for those that are not too obtrusive. The most popular colours for general gardening are white, green and brown; in an alpine garden situation it is better to go for those that have been made to look like natural stone.

When in full alpine glory, these containers can make very effective focal points. They are, of course, ideal for standing on a patio, path, driveway, or next to a door. But they can also look very good when stood in borders. The tubs, raised slightly on blocks, can be placed in a part of the garden that is not at its best when the plants in the tub are at their prettiest.

Siting containers

Unless you intend to grow just shade-loving plants in the container, it is best to site it in an open position in full sun. To get the most pleasure out of your container it should be put in places that are frequently visited, such as on the edge of a patio, path or driveway. A firm, paved (or at least level) base is desirable.

Ideally the container is best raised off the ground a little. This will ensure that the drainage works and will prevent worms, slugs and weeds working their way in through the drainage holes. Four bricks, in a single layer at each corner of the container, will be sufficient, but two layers of bricks will be even better as then leaves and debris that collect underneath can be removed.

↗ **Alpine and bedding plant mix**
This square plastic container sitting on a gravel driveway contains a mix of alpines and tender bedding plants.

↗ **Sink in a sunny position**
Free-standing alpine containers such as this sink need to be placed in an open, sunny position. This planting scheme has a small conifer within it to provide height.

It may be possible to make attractive groupings of two or more containers on a patio or terrace. I have also seen instances where owners have removed one or two paving stones in order to plant the area around the base of the container, to make more of an alpine feature.

COMPOST AND ROCKS

Place drainage crocks or other drainage material (large pieces of gravel, polystyrene chips, etc) in the bottom of the container, to a depth of some 1½ –2in (4–5cm). Then cover this with a layer of polythene membrane, the sort that is used as an outdoor fabric mulch. It contains holes so that water can percolate through.

On top of this will go the compost. This should be a mixture of 1 part (by volume) of loam, 1 part of peat, coir or leafmould, and 2 parts grit. Add a small handful of general fertilizer such as bonemeal or fish, blood and bone. An alternative to this mixture would be to use 1 part of John Innes (JI) No. 3 potting compost, to 1 part grit.

You can make up your own compost, which involves mixing quantities of loam, peat, coarse sand, ground chalk, hoof and horn meal, superphosphate of lime and sulphate of potash – the recipe is available on the internet, but you would need to purchase sterilized loam or sterilize your own loam at home – which is not something the average gardener would wish to do. Whichever compost you have chosen for your alpine sink or trough, press it down well.

The planting

There are many small plants that will enjoy the free-drainage conditions that a trough will provide. As with the larger rockery garden, it is possible to provide pockets of different compost to suit certain types of plants. Thus it is possible to increase the amount of moisture-retaining humus in some areas, particularly on the shady sides of rocks, so that a few plants such as some forms of *Gentiana* and *Primula* may be grown.

Do not use plants that will grow too big: small cushion plants or those that gently spread to form small mats are best. Variations can be made using small shrubs and conifers, as well as a few trailing plants over the side.

Avoid planting your alpines too deep and too high; also, do not damage the roots during the planting process, firm plants in place and water them immediately.

The final touch is to apply a top-dressing to the surface of the compost, between the rocks and the plants. It is best to use chippings that are in sympathy with the rocks, and to avoid, for example, limestone chippings with sandstone rocks. Coloured nuggets, gravel and chippings are available these days, but they are better suited to covering contemporary garden containers, not naturalistic alpine containers.

Slate chippings are available in grey, plum, green and bluish colours. These can look effective in an alpine garden situation, but use them with caution in an alpine container as the chippings can be quite large and appear out of scale with the landscape in the container.

ALPINE TIP

Most containers look better if they also have some rocks added to them. This is not only a decorative feature, but also provides the plants with a cool root-run, some protection from the sun and, for those planted in crevices, even more acute drainage. These rocks can be of any type. It is nice to have several containers, each with different kinds of rock – some may be rugged, others rounded, and yet others may be jagged or fissured. These rocks should be well buried into the compost with only the top half or less showing above the surface.

↗ **Ceramic bowl**

A neutral-coloured ceramic bowl makes a fine container for a patio or table-top alpine feature.

↗ **Top-dressing**

When planted, finish off with a top-dressing of gravel (in this case coloured white) and some larger pieces of stone.

↗ **Watering**

The final stage in planting an alpine container is to water the plants in, using a watering can with a fine rose-end attachment, to prevent washing the compost away with powerful spurts of water.

↗ **Instant feature**

The completed container in its final resting place. Note how several plants that are already in flower have been used; this means that the container becomes an instant feature, without having to wait for it to look good.

06

THE ALPINE HOUSE

Alpines under cover

Sooner or later, all alpine enthusiasts will yearn for
an alpine house where they can display their plants,
protected from winter wetness and cold.

WHAT IS AN ALPINE HOUSE?

As explained on page 26, an alpine house is a specialized form of greenhouse, and its sole purpose is to protect alpine plants from rain and sometimes excessive cold. Of course, it is perfectly possible to grow alpines and become an alpine enthusiast without having an alpine house, but sooner or later most collectors yearn to own one. It enables them to increase the range and scope of plants in a collection, as well as to display them in a most attractive way.

Alpine houses can be purchased from specialist firms, but most growers find that the expense of such a house is beyond their means and instead make do with a modified greenhouse. The main modification will be to the ventilation (in that an alpine house needs much more of it).

↑ Alpine house in winter

This picture was taken in mid-winter, when most of the garden outside was bleak and colourless. Inside the alpine house it is a riot of colour.

← Alpine house

With an interesting selection of plants and some careful planning, an alpine house can be full of colour all year round.

How is it designed?

The traditional alpine house is built with solid walls of brick or stone up to bench level and then glazed above. Many of the older houses were built into the ground with a central walkway that was excavated into the soil and with the glazing rising off low foundations just above ground level.

The advantage of this is that the ground acts as a storage heater and the alpine house is warmer at night. Because the structure is lower, it is not so prone to being chilled by the wind; however, there is the risk of the floors flooding after heavy rain.

These days most greenhouses are glazed to the ground. This is fine for alpines, except the house is more likely to suffer extremes of temperature. This means that some form of insulation, such as bubble plastic, is best used during the winter. This should be adhered to the inside of the glazing but only below the staging level, as alpine plants need bright winter light.

Purpose-built alpine houses have a low 'pitch', which brings the plants as near as possible to the glass. However, the steeper 'pitch' of a traditional greenhouse is not a particularly serious drawback.

Traditionally the flooring is a straight line from the end door to the 'back' of the house, but if the house is large there is no reason why a curved pathway could not snake its way across the length of the house. However, this would then require a degree of innovation when it comes to the staging. Curved staging is not easy to construct, but it is possible.

The flooring should be firm, stable, level and easy to clean. On this basis you can do no better than to create a raft of concrete. An alternative method is to put down paving slabs. These have the advantage in that they can be taken up and moved if necessary.

↗ **Modern greenhouse**
Modern greenhouses have glass to the ground. This is not a problem for alpine houses, but traditionally they are half-brick affairs, meaning that they are slightly better insulated in winter.

↗ **Concrete flooring**
The flooring in the alpine house should be level and sturdy. Most popular types are flat rafts of concrete laid on a firm foundation or, as seen here, slabs that have the benefit of being moveable after time.

ALPINE TIP

When choosing an alpine house, go for the largest house you can afford and that your site will allow. What may seem to be a large structure when empty, soon becomes filled to capacity with plants. Remember to properly view alpine plants when they are in full flower, there needs to be enough space between each one.

What should it be made from?

The same types of materials are available for alpine houses as greenhouses. You can choose between aluminium, wood or UPVC for the main structure, and glass or clear plastic for glazing.

Wood has many advantages, for example, in cold weather it is marginally warmer than metal, and in high windy weather it is just a little stronger (metal is prone to bending). Also, wood seems to fit into the landscape better than a metal greenhouse. The disadvantages of wood can be summed up in terms of cost and maintenance. The initial outlay is greater than aluminium, by quite some degree.

In terms of maintenance, most wooden houses are made from cedar, which is relatively long-lasting – but only if treated well. Cheaper wooden houses will be made from a softer wood and will not last as long. Once a year the outside-facing wood – of whichever type – should be treated by rubbing with a wire brush to remove flaking paint or varnish and then a new coat applied.

UPVC is a modern material and is long lasting but expensive. It generally comes in white, although other colours are available, such as dark green. The maintenance required to look after UPVC is not great – another advantage – but it would pay you to look over it at least once a year to check for holes or degradation.

Aluminium houses are cheap and easier to maintain. Also, the glazing bars are usually thinner, so let in more sunlight. They are, however, not the most attractive of structures, and many gardeners prefer the other options.

As for the glazing, there are glass and clear plastic options. Glass always has been and continues to be the preferred option. It is sturdy, long-lasting and light-transmissive. Clear plastic degrades in time and is easily scratched.

↗ **Low pitch greenhouse**
This aluminium alpine house has a low, wider span than most greenhouses, meaning that the plants on benches are closer to the glass.

↗ **Coloured metal frames**
Modern metal alpine (and green) houses can be bought in colours; dark green is, perhaps, the most appropriate for a garden situation.

Where should it be sited?

Ideally, alpine houses should be placed with an east-west run. This means that the plants on the inside receive maximum light from the winter sun. However, this does not have to be adhered to strictly and if, by necessity, a house has to run north-south, it is useful to have the door (if only at one end) at the end that faces the sun.

In fact, shade (and light transmission generally) is the most important factor. It is advisable to keep alpine houses in the open, away from any shade. However, there are some alpine enthusiasts – and I am one of them – that have adopted a rather radical and innovative approach. My alpine house is under an open tree (an apple) that produces light, dappled shade. During the winter when maximum light is required, there are no leaves on the tree. Then, later in the year when the sun becomes stronger, automatic shading is produced by the leaves as they open. This works fine as long as the leaves of the tree in question do not become too dense.

Of course on a bright day in summer, the sun shines straight through, especially at certain angles, so part shading (see page 71) applied to the glass may be necessary.

The two downsides to tree shading that I have experienced are that on a dull, cloudy day in summer it can be quite dark and dingy in the alpine house, and also that falling apples have broken two panes of glass! However, I have persisted with it and now tend to pick in advance the apples that are in danger of causing damage as they get heavier.

↗ **Part-shaded greenhouse**
Site alpine houses east-west. This way is most light-efficient, as the sun will be shining along the length of the house for the greater part of the day.

↗ **Shading by an apple tree**
Houses set under trees with a semi-dense canopy (this is an apple tree, viewed in winter) have some form of automatic shading in summer when the leaves are out.

ALPINE TIP

It is worth laying a path from your residence to the alpine house, if there isn't one already. It will be well used in winter, when the ground may frequently be wet or frozen and a properly constructed path will be much better.

DISPLAYING YOUR ALPINES

You can, if you wish, grow alpines on the floor of the alpine house, but most people prefer to install some form of benching, which not only brings the plants up to a convenient height for tending and viewing, but also means that there is space beneath the staging for storing dormant plants. A further layer of staging can be built below the main staging, giving a wide shelf, then the ground itself can be used for more storage.

Any normal greenhouse staging is fine if all you are intending to do is to display plants; the exception is if you intend to have a plunging bed (see opposite). Home-made wooden slatted staging seems conducive to alpine growing, but technically there is no reason why metal bench staging, sold by standard greenhouse retailers, should not be used. The most convenient working height for the staging should be around waist high, which is about 30in (76cm). The depth of the staging, from front to back, should not exceed the distance that you can reach, bearing in mind you may have to lift heavy pots right to the back.

Plunging

Some people like to 'plunge' their alpine pots into sand up to the bottom of their neck bands. For this the staging needs to be built on a sturdy base, with high sides in order to accommodate a 6–8in (15–20cm) deep bed of sand. The purpose of the plunge method is twofold. First, it can prevent pots from drying out too quickly and secondly it helps prevent them freezing in winter. It mainly benefits clay pots (which have porous sides), but even plants in plastic pots benefit from this extra winter protection.

Use sharp sand for the plunging material; if you add a bulking substance to this (such as peat or coir, in a ratio of 1 part bulking material to 2 parts sand) then when a pot is removed for any reason, its hole does not cave in, making it difficult to replace or re-create. The only downside to adding the bulking material is that it can encourage the growth of moss.

I do not personally plunge, but if I did, I would not use bulking material because of the potential moss growth; as long as the sand is not allowed to dry out, replacing pots into their original holes should not be too much of a problem.

↗ **Wooden staging**
Wooden slatted staging is convenient, cheap and effective.

↗ **Bench staging**
Bench staging with capillary matting means that the plants are less likely to be overwatered, and they stand out well against the white material.

↗ Plunging

Sharp sand is the usual material for a plunge bed, although sometimes gardeners like to mix peat with it so that it retains its shape better when plants are removed.

↗ Raised beds

Raised beds can also be landscaped, with lumps of rock representing mountain scapes.

Raised beds

One step further on from plunge beds are raised beds. These are beds raised off the floor where alpine plants can be planted into the soil and also where their roots can be allowed to spread unhindered – rather like an extended trough under cover. The bed can be flat and designed and planted up in much the same way as a sink garden. Or, because it offers a larger area in which to create an alpine landscape, you can give it a scree-like slope or accommodate larger rocks to give the appearance of a mountain scape, albeit in miniature. The only limiting factor here is the weight – if heavy rocks are being used, then the raised beds need to be sturdily built.

Landscaping

The final way to display plants in an alpine house is to incorporate them into landscaped beds. This is similar to the raised-bed method above, but carried out at floor level. There is likely to be more room for this than you have with a raised bed and there is no limiting weight factor. Therefore anything goes!

↗ Storage space

With carefully constructed benching there is usually plenty of space beneath for extra shelving and storage.

↗ Landscaping

This is a landscaped scree bed inside an alpine house, with the rear of the landscaped area rising up to half the height of the sides of the house.

VENTILATION

You must get the ventilation right. The more air – of moderate intensity, not gale-force winds – that passes through an alpine house the better. Air movement helps to cool plants down in warm weather and, more importantly, prevents fungal rots that become most troublesome in damp, stagnant air. If possible, there should be vents along each side of the house, all along the roof ridge, and opening doors at each end. This may seem excessive, but true alpine plants will be all the better for it.

The large amount of ventilation does not, unfortunately, apply to ordinary standard greenhouses, but these can be adapted at relatively little extra cost. Most greenhouses are manufactured by the unit system, meaning that it is possible to purchase extra vents, which can then be inserted in place of the normal glazing. If money is tight, you could even remove whole panes of glass from a standard greenhouse when the weather is warm, and replace them as it cools at the end of the season. The trouble with this, of course, is that the plants sitting directly beneath a 'hole' in the greenhouse roof such as this will be subjected to rain, hail and all the other elements.

↗ **Ridge ventilation**
The importance of good ventilation cannot be over-emphasized. Here, ridge vents run all the way along the length of the alpine house.

↗ **Simple vents**
With a much smaller alpine house or a greenhouse the vents may be simple hinged panes and fasteners.

↗ **Side vents**
Louvred vents are normally installed in the sides of an alpine house; they provide plenty of through-draft for the plants.

SHADING

The hot sun from late spring onwards will be too strong for most alpines growing under glass. The rise in temperature can be addressed by the opening of the vents, but the intensity of the light can only be controlled by the use of shading.

There are three main types of shading: whitening that is brushed on like paint; netting on rolls or frames that are clipped on to the glazing bars; and a roll of wooden battens or metal or plastic laths that can be rolled up and down.

The whitening is the cheapest form of shading, and for some is the most convenient. However, there are several disadvantages to it. First, it is applied in late spring or early summer and remains there until it is wiped off at some point during the autumn. Therefore on dull, overcast days in summer it can create quite a dingy look to the interior of the alpine house. It can also be difficult to apply to some of the higher panels and is quite a messy job.

Netting is not too expensive, but suppliers of ready-made netting panels may be difficult to find and, although they can be put up and taken down at will, this can be cumbersome.

Without doubt the most useful and the most attractive form of shading is a roller, which can be raised and lowered by simple pulleys – a job that takes seconds to do. They are quick and effective – but also the most expensive.

← **Whitening**
Paint-on shading is the cheapest and, for some, most convenient form of shading. But it can render the inside of the alpine house dingy on dull, overcast days.

↗ **Roller shading and side vents**
Here, sophisticated side vents have been designed to co-exist with roller lath shading.

ALPINE TIPS
||||||||||||||||||||||||||||||||||||||||||||||||||||||||||||||||||||||||||||||

To keep temperatures down, shading must always be on the outside of the glazing. For example, if net shading is put up on the inside, the sun's light has already penetrated the glass before it hits the shading material and has therefore already heated up part of the inside environment.

Make sure the shading system does not interfere with the effectiveness of the ventilators. There is no point in installing the correct number of vents if the free-flow of air through these vents is blocked by close-mesh netting or roller laths. These forms of shading should, therefore, be set just below the level of the roof vents.

WHAT ABOUT HEATING?

The one question that provokes more argument between alpine gardeners than probably any other subject is that of whether an alpine house should be heated (see page 27). The house at Wisley had 'Bernie the boiler', a coal-fired boiler that was used to heat water pipes so that the house remained free of frost. I believe that the main function of an alpine house is to keep moisture out while maintaining a free flow of air. In a motoring context I liken an alpine house to a car port, whereas a heated greenhouse is more like an enclosed garage.

For this reason I do not personally advocate heating alpine houses. This practice was mostly carried out a hundred years ago, in the belief that plants needed to be kept frost-free. We now understand better that in most cases it is not the frost that is the killer, but exposure to prolonged winter moisture.

Certainly if you take into account the costs of fuel and energy, it is questionable whether you get value for money in heating an alpine house. What is more pertinent, however, is that it should accommodate alpine plants only and should not also be used for the growing of tender plants. The differences in conditions needed for growing are likely to be very different and the result could be the loss of one genre of plants, or even both.

← **Perspex cold frame**
These cold frames have sides made of Perspex to allow in more light.

COLD FRAMES

Before we leave the subject of growing alpine plants under cover, we should take a look at the value of cold frames. These frames are able to undertake most of the functions of a full-sized alpine house, except accommodate the gardener!

Frames have the advantage of being cheaper than an alpine house; they can offer 100 per cent ventilation in summer by removal of the lids; they can be completely covered during particularly cold spells in winter by closing the frames; and being low to the ground, they are not so obtrusive in the garden.

Their main function is the same as an alpine house, specifically to provide protection against the elements for plants in pots. However, they are more often than not used by alpine gardeners as a storage area for plants that are not in flower, or are resting; these plants, when 'in season' are then taken into the alpine house for their main displays. They may also be used for housing young or recently propagated plants. For these reasons, cold frames should be used in addition to an alpine house, rather than instead of one.

Similar principles of shading and ventilation as discussed for alpine houses apply to cold frames, but these structures are not generally used for pure display, so you are unlikely to see them landscaped or containing large rocks.

← **Brick cold frame**
It is important that cold frames should be allowed to open wide, or to have the 'lights' (lids) removed completely in warm weather.

CHAPTER

07

YEAR-ROUND MAINTENANCE

Water good idea!

Waterfalls and cascades can make a wonderful feature of the rock garden – but remember that a water course such as this will need to be maintained throughout the year.

↘

SEASONAL JOBS

Any experienced alpine gardener will tell you that there are things to do every month of the year – in fact, every week of the year. There are, of course, several jobs that need doing whenever they are necessary and regardless of the season. Included here are tasks such as weeding, watering plants when they are dry, looking out for pests and diseases, deadheading, the removal of dead plants, and the regular checking of ponds and rockery water courses to ensure they are not getting clogged with algae.

   This chapter also covers those jobs that are season-specific. We have divided the alpine gardening year into 12 sub-seasons rather than months, as the weather can vary considerably in different regions for each month.

↗ Vine weevil larvae
The larvae of vive weevils are found in the compost from potted and containerized plants during winter. These grubs have a particular liking for cyclamen, but many other plants, too. They eat the roots and corms of susceptible plants, which can eventually kill them.

↓ Heathers
A rock garden, seen here with a range of heathers, will not look after itself; there is maintenance to undertake and jobs to do every week of the year.

EARLY WINTER

General hygiene and pest eradication

Amongst a plethora of insect pests that can attack our garden plants, the following two are particularly troublesome with alpines. At this time of year you need to look for grubs lurking in the soil and overwintering adults and eggs.

Vine weevils: The grubs of these beetle-like creatures eat into the roots of plants growing in pots or other containers, outdoors or under cover. Plants growing in the open ground are less likely to be damaged, but it is still possible – they have a particular liking for *Cyclamen* corms. The grubs devour the roots, and plants wilt and die when attacked, which occurs most commonly from early winter to late spring, and again in early autumn. During summer the adult weevils eat irregular-shaped holes in leaf margins.

The main control available to gardeners is a chemical called imidacloprid; it is available in various formulations for spraying directly on to plants or impregnated in potting compost as a preventative measure.

Aphids: Greenfly or blackfly feed by sucking the sap of young, tender plant growths, and they are often seen clustering on young, unopened buds and also on the undersides of young leaves. Their feeding will not kill an established plant, unless it is very small, but it will distort the buds and leaves, which can ruin the appearance as well as the flowering and possibly the fruiting potential.

Aphids also excrete a sugary substance called 'honeydew', which can be further infected by a black fungus called sooty mould. In severe cases this will prevent the sun's light from reaching the green parts of the plant.

Small aphid infestations seen over-wintering on alpines should be cut off the plants and thrown away. However, this is not really practical for very small plants, so you should be prepared to spray these. There are many suitable insecticides on the market to choose from.

Repotting

Make an early start if any of your alpines need repotting. It is a good idea to check forms of *Primula* first, as these will be becoming active first (in fact, some of the *Vernales* primulas will already be in bloom). Leave anything that is flowering until immediately after the flowers have faded before you repot the plants.

The process for repotting alpines is as follows:

1. Before removing a plant from its pot, clean it up. Remove any dead leaves (tweezers may be needed for this).
2. Gently turn the plant out of its pot; if there is a mass of roots it could benefit from repotting. If there is not a mass of roots, place it back into the same pot.
3. If it needs repotting, gently work away some of the soil so that the outer roots hang free.
4. Repot in a similar sized or slightly larger pot, introducing fresh compost (of the same mix as described on page 60) between the roots and leaving as little root disturbed as possible.

Build a rocky outcrop

If major garden construction needs to take place, this is the time to do it, while much of the garden is lying dormant. Of course, building a rockery, a rocky outcrop, raised beds or a full-scale rock garden, can be carried out at any time of year, but now is when the upheaval and mess caused by heavy construction is least likely to cause you a problem. Descriptions of construction are discussed in chapter 4.

↘

MID-WINTER

Watch for slugs

In surveys of amateur gardeners the slug is the creature that frequently ranks as the number one pest. In a rockery garden these slimy molluscs are highly troublesome as they like to hide under the stone where it is cool and moist.

Slugs and snails will readily munch their way through the soft, fleshy leaves and stems of seedlings, as well as many types of soft adult alpines. They seem to leave cyclamen and primulas alone, but tend to enjoy many members of the daisy family and young bulbs.

Rockery gardens that have been topped with sharp grade shingle may be left alone, as the slugs find it difficult to slide over such inhospitable material.

Poisonous baits based on metaldehyde or methiocarb can be applied in small quantities to the ground near to susceptible plants, but if possible try to use less toxic remedies.

Dividing overgrown clumps

Between now and late spring is the best time to divide overgrown clumps of alpines, or you can wait for the two or three-week period in early autumn. Most alpines are small and can be pulled apart by hand. Many forms of *Campanula*, *Iris*, *Primula*, *Sedum*, *Sempervivum* and *Thymus*, can be divided. *Gentiana* tends to fall apart very easily, while *Hepatica* takes a bit more effort.

How to divide an alpine:

1. Lift the clump out of the ground, or turn an overgrown plant out of its pot.
2. In the case of bulbous plants, you can gently separate the bulbs by hand. With a herbaceous alpine that has lots of fibrous roots and several crowns, work your fingers and thumbs into the heart of the plant and firmly but gently try to prise it into sections. If this is not feasible you may need to dip the plant into a bucket of water and work the soil away and the roots apart; then the individual plants can be more easily separated. Some forms of *Iris* and *Primula* may need to be cut with a clean knife.
3. With larger clumps there will be an old, central portion of plant that is of no use. This should be discarded.
4. Repot or plant out the new sections.

← **Slugs**
The slug is the number one pest for many gardeners. It is most dangerous for young plants and seedlings, however, it can ravage many different plants, including alpines. Slugs do tend to avoid hairy-leaved plants, however.

↑ Fertilizing
Unlike bedding plants and fruits and vegetables, alpine plants are not generally hungry – after all, they do tend to live in high, mountainous crags where there is little nutrition in the meagre soil they inhabit. However, a yearly feed with a general fertilizer is usually well received, especially if the plant is free-flowering.

Feed – where needed

Alpines, generally, are not hungry plants. They do, after all, come from rocky crags, crevices and such like where there is unlikely to be very much highly fertile soil. In our gardens, plants grown directly in the ground – on a rockery, say – will require less feeding than those grown in pots or containers.

However, if you grow lots of plants on a rockery, particularly plants known for their energy-using flowers, then the soil can quickly become depleted of goodness. Feed by putting down a little granular general fertilizer, such as Growmore, applied according to manufacturers' recommendations, and then lightly hoed or forked in. Organic gardeners can use bonemeal, fishmeal or seaweed-based fertilizer.

ALPINE TIP

To get rid of slugs try putting down orange peel, which attracts them in numbers where they can be collected and disposed of, or beer traps, where they are lured into a slop-trough of beer and drown. I have also tried biological controls – nematodes that you water onto the soil. All can work, but there are no guarantees.

LATE WINTER

Sow seeds

Usually seed of alpine plants is sown as soon as it is ripe, and this is likely to be in the summer or autumn. However, quite a large proportion of seed that has fallen to the ground in the wild is programmed to wait for frost to come before it germinates. So for the alpine gardener now is a good time to sow seeds of these plants, and leave them to the weather outside. Frosts are likely to trigger germination, after which the pots can be moved into a cold frame or unheated greenhouse, where the seedlings will grow on strongly and not suffer from prolonged winter wet.

Planting and potting new alpines

This is the time of year when the alpine gardener is most intent on wanting to buy something new. This is partly due to the fact that now is the best time for planting. The soil is warming and young plants are likely to grow away quickly, giving reasonably instant effect and pleasure. There should be plenty of rain over the coming months, with neither high temperatures nor drought to cause distress to the plants. Planting advice is given on pages 44–5.

Remove winter cover

By now it is normally safe to remove the glass or plastic sheeting (or any other form of artificial cover) that has been protecting alpines from excessive winter wet. See Late Autumn (page 96).

ALPINE TIP

Beware: if you know a seed is likely to be highly fertile, it is a huge mistake to sow too much. Just a pinch of seed between your finger and thumb would suffice. Growing too many seedlings means you either have the heartbreaking decision to throw away the surplus or give them away. Worse still, you may be tempted to keep them, pot them up, and then for the rest of the year you have to care for a population of plants you do not really want.

↗ Sowing alpines
Late winter is a good time for sowing seeds of alpine plants. It is often the case that alpine seeds need to be subjected to frost and cold conditions before they will germinate, therefore sowing now, and leaving the pots outside to experience even one frost is likely to assist germination.

⬈ Weeding

As elsewhere in the garden, when weeds grow they compete with cultivated plants for soil goodness, space, light and moisture. On a rock garden they can also quickly impose themselves on small alpine plants. Therefore a good session of weeding in early spring, before growth really gets underway, will pay dividends.

EARLY SPRING

Weeding

Weeds fall into two main categories. The first are the annuals, which propagate themselves by seeding from the mature plants, and which only last one year. Then there are the perennials, which spread by the roots and shoots that creep along the ground, and which persist from year to year. They also set seed and propagate themselves by this method, too.

The easiest weeds to control are annuals; in the open garden these are best kept in check by hand-weeding, hoeing, mulching and spraying. The perennial weeds, such as ground elder, couch grass (or twitch), bindweed, as well as daisies, dandelions and docks, will need to be dug out and completely removed from the soil by hand, or sprayed with a potent herbicide (such as the ones based on glyphosate) that kills the plant completely. A weedkiller containing glyphosate will be able to do this, but you must make sure not to get it onto any nearby plants that you wish to keep, as it will kill them too.

Top-dressing

Top-dress the rock garden now to keep it looking tidy. By following this guide you can quickly and effectively give your alpine area a new look:

1. Rake off loose gravel, slate or chippings that are currently in place.
2. Pull out weeds and lift unwanted plants, or any that have outgrown their space.
3. Loosen the top 2–3in (5–7.5cm) of soil and finely rake it over to improve the desired contours.
4. Add a little fresh compost (the mix is described on page 60), and rake to the desired contours.
5. Dust with fertilizer (see page 79).
6. Finish by sprinkling, placing or shovelling new chippings, gravel or slate on to the soil. If there is room, rake it to a smooth surface.

MID-SPRING

Watering and mulching

As the weather warms up, watering can become essential. This is even more important with plants that have been recently planted. Throughout this book so far I have mentioned the importance of good drainage where alpines are concerned, as most types perish if their roots are sitting in water. But one of the disadvantages of using a free-draining compost is that in dry and warm weather there is very little water retention, and the plants can quickly dehydrate.

Watering is best carried out either early in the day or in the evening – both times when the sun is low in the sky and evaporation will be at its slowest.

↘ Watering
Whereas alpine plants do not need a constantly moist soil like many other garden plants, it is important that they do not suffer dryness for long periods. Rockeries are usually free-draining structures, which means that when the weather starts to warm up you should check for dryness regularly, and apply water when needed.

A good soaking every few days in hot weather is better for plants – and less wasteful of water. Alpines grown in containers, such as sinks and troughs, tend to dry out quickly as they are not in the ground where there is more moisture available generally, and they are usually placed in a sunny, open position.

If you have a great number of containers and pots, or an alpine house, and there is a chance you are likely to be away during warm weather, automatic watering systems can be installed, to irrigate plants in your absence. These devices are attached to a mains water tap and the pipes run along the areas for watering. A timer mechanism at the tap end can be activated at a pre-set time.

The water exits from these pipes either through 'seep holes', or from stand-pipes with a jet nozzle to regulate the spray and its direction of coverage. The seep-hole system allows water to gently trickle through holes at intervals along the length of the pipes to soak the ground.

ALPINE TIP

In the open garden, organic mulches can prevent rapid loss of soil moisture, however, on a rock garden, they are not so welcome. They tend to enrich the soil too much for alpines, they can smother plants (which in alpines is likely to cause rapid death) and it just looks horrible. Instead, slate chippings, gravel or grit are the materials of choice. If you don't have any on your rock garden, apply it now.

Take stem cuttings – softwood

A number of alpines can be propagated now by taking softwood cuttings of the stems. Shoot lengths should be between 1–3in (2.5–8cm) depending on the plant (some will not be able to offer you stems at the longer end of this range). Plants that may be increased by softwood stem cuttings at this time include *Andromeda*, *Campanula*, *Erodium*, *Iberis*, *Saxifraga*, *Thymus* and *Veronica*.

How to take cuttings:

1. With a pair of secateurs or a sharp knife, cut healthy shoots of new growth from the plant.
2. Nip off or cut off the lower leaves, leaving about 1in (2.5cm) of clean stem.
3. Dip the very bottom tip of the cutting into hormone rooting powder, and gently tap off excess powder.
4. Insert the cutting into a tray or small pot that contains moist compost of equal parts grit and peat or coir.
5. If the cuttings are in a pot, enclose the pot in a clear polythene bag, bound with a rubber band. This maintains a high level of humidity around the cuttings. If in a tray, it is advisable to place this in a propagating frame, or under a domed lid that can come with some trays, so that the humidity level is improved.
6. Place pot or tray in a warmish spot, away from direct sunshine. A sign of successful rooting will be visible new growth after a few weeks.

LATE SPRING

Trimming and deadheading

At the beginning of the growing year a rock-garden border should be tidied up. Old, dying top-growth should be cut back to ground level. Use secateurs for the thicker stems, and a pair of hand shears for lighter shoots. Try to remove the stems as closely as possible to the crowns of clumpy plants.

Deadheading is the removal of faded flowers from a plant before it has produced the seed. All cultivated flowering plants should be dead-headed: you will save the plant a huge amount of wasted energy, and you will either encourage more flowers in the same year or help to build up the plant for better flowering the following year.

Generally with alpines the recommendation is to use a pair of secateurs and to cut off the faded flowers, cutting the stalks down as far as the first set of leaves. As always there are exceptions. Dwarf rhododendrons, for example, should have their old flowerheads snapped off with your fingers. Sub-shrubs, such as heathers can be deadheaded with shears.

Deadheading now will apply to those alpines that have recently finished flowering, but also to any plants that flowered over the winter and which were not deadheaded at the time because by leaving the faded flowers in place the area was more decorative at a dull time or year, or because they were of use to visiting birds and other wildlife.

Shading, ventilation and watering

There are periods of bright sunshine now and this can be too strong for certain plants, such as *Primula*, *Hepatica*, *Ramonda* and *Rhodohypoxis*. It is time, therefore, to put the shading option of your choice (see page 71) into effect.

Adequate ventilation should be applied to alpine plants the year round, but it can become critical in alpine houses from now on. If you are out at work all day and do not possess automatic ventilation, then open all of the vents before you leave for the day and then shut them back up again in the evening.

Similarly, the watering of alpine plants under glass can be critical now. Depending on the heat, watering may need to be carried out every day from now until early autumn.

Take leaf cuttings

This is a method of propagating some plants, most notably *Haberlea*, *Ramonda* and *Sedum*. Here's how:

1. Select a leaf, or a leaf of a rosette that is young but has reached a good size.
2. Gently pull it sideways, holding it at the base of its stalk. The aim is to detach the leaf with the complete stalk right down to its junction with the main stem; it is at this point that there is a cluster of cells, or an incipient bud, that is able to produce a new growing point. It is possible for parts of the stalk higher up to root, but it is unlikely to produce a growing point, therefore is likely to fail.
3. Insert the detached leaf, stalk downwards, into a compost mixture (as described on page 60). Insert at a narrow angle with the leaf blade almost flush with the surface of the compost. The whole of the stalk and up to a third of the leaf blade should be covered, but ensure that leaves of neighbouring cuttings are not touching each other.
4. Mist spray the pot or tray, and treat as for stem cuttings (page 83). Young plants should have developed sufficiently by the end of summer, at which time they can be potted up.

Stem cuttings – softwood and semi-ripe

By now there will be many more alpine plants producing growths suitable for cuttings. The aim should always be to get cuttings rooted and established as independent plants before the onset of winter. With some plants the growth will still be very soft and pliable, but in others the shoots may be turning slightly woody – this is called semi-ripe wood.

Plants that can be propagated by this method and at this time include *Aethionema*, *Dianthus*, *Helianthemum* and *Phlox*. Instructions on how to take stem cuttings appear on page 83.

↗ **Trimming**

One of the jobs that should be carried out as and when it is needed is that of trimming and deadheading. Winter- and early spring-flowering plants will now be over, so late spring is therefore a good time to trim and tidy these plants.

EARLY SUMMER

Preparations for holidays

Summer is when many of us go on holiday for a week or two. But plants may still need attention, even if you are not there to give it. Before you go, attend to the following:

Watering: Make sure that your most precious plants are thoroughly watered each day for at least three days before you set off. Moisture will accumulate in the soil around the roots and it will penetrate deeper as well, so the bottom-most roots will be able to suck it up, even if a hot period of weather dries out the top part of the soil. Consider installing a drip watering system – either to water your plants in pots, your alpine house or the entire garden. A system can be rigged up to an outside tap and controlled by a timing device, which can be set to come on and go off at certain times.

Weeding: Thoroughly weed the rockery areas; weeds compete with your garden plants for moisture.

Mulches: Around your rock plants the mulch of gravel or grit should be topped up to prevent evaporation of soil moisture.

Alpine house: Obviously you should water plants inside thoroughly for a couple of days before you depart, but do not apply any fertilizer at these times, as it will make the plants grow and use up more water while you're away. Leave the door and vents open wide, to give the maximum air circulation. Professional plant growers sometimes use sophisticated air conditioning units and air-cooling fans in large greenhouses, but opening the doors and vents is all you can sensibly do to keep potentially high midday temperatures at bay. Just as important is the question of shade. Give the plants inside your alpine house relief from the sun by putting up some form of shading (see page 71).

Containers: Any alpines in moveable containers should be stood in a shady corner of the garden.

Cut off flowers: This may sound crazy, but if you cut off some of the flower heads – dead or alive – from plants (especially those in sinks or other containers), it will help to prolong the lives of the plants by stopping them from 'wasting' energy in producing flowers that no-one will see! You could even come back to bushier, sturdier plants that will flower later than normal.

⬈ Timing device

If you are employing a sprinkler or drip irrigation system on your rock garden or in your alpine house, control is essential if water is not to be wasted. Using a timer-controlled water valve enables a regular watering regime to be established.

Neighbours: You can always beg, plead, implore and beseech your neighbours to do whatever they can to keep everything running smoothly during your absence. If this isn't possible you could take a winter holiday instead!

← Mulching a rhododendron

To conserve soil moisture and help to prevent further weed growth, top up mulching around plants. At the back of a rockery, thicker, organic mulching materials such as bark and well-rotted compost may be used. Towards the front of the rockery, where the smaller and more delicate alpine plants are likely to be seen, it is common practice to use gravel, grit or chippings.

MID–SUMMER

Repotting bulbs

Mid-summer is traditionally the time for shaking out spring-flowering potted bulbs, sorting them and repotting them. Many small bulbs can be left for two years in the same pot, with only a small change of compost in the top 1in (2.5cm) or so. But for those that need repotting, follow this guide:

1. Prepare a potting compost mixture of 3 parts John Innes No. 2 potting compost, 2 parts of coarse grit or sand, and 1 part peat or coir. Add a pinch or two of bonemeal fertilizer per pot if you are potting larger bulbs.

2. Empty a pot of old, flowered bulbs – with dying or dead foliage – on to a clear bench.

3. Scrape away the soil mixture to reveal the bulbs, collecting them all together.

4. Check the bulbs over, discarding any that are showing signs of pest or disease, or are damaged, or clearly dead. Clean off loose scales (sometimes known as 'tunics') and detach any loose offsets (small 'baby' bulbs growing alongside the mother bulb).

5. Replant the good, healthy bulbs in the fresh compost. Use large pots for the larger bulbs, and small for small. As for depth, follow the guidance given on page 90.

ALPINE TIP

If you are not able to plant your bulbs straight away, store them in a cool, dry place, never near heaters – and never in plastic bags as this makes them sweat. Open any bags before planting to let air circulate.

← Bulbs by post

Bulbs sent in the mail usually come in 'breathable' polythene bags. If they don't, open the bags so that the bulbs can breathe.

Buy bulbs for spring flowering

Confusingly, bulbs, tubers and corms are all often described as 'bulbs'. All three are basic storage organs for the plant, containing a supply of water and food that keeps the plant alive while it is dormant; however, most tubers and corms are actually modified, swollen stems.

Most people think of bulbs in the garden as the spring-flowering types, such as daffodils (*Narcissus*), tulips, crocuses, hyacinths and so on. Mid-summer is when garden centres become well stocked with them. At the same time the first of the new season's mail-order bulb catalogues will be sent out to customers. Although the following spring may seem a long way off, ordering early has many advantages: those bulbs that require early planting, such as *Narcissus* will be with you

in good time; also, if you delay ordering, then some varieties may be sold out by later in the season. When selecting bulbs from a shop, avoid any that do not have a clean base, or that are soft and show signs of rot. Avoid any, too, that have started to shoot, producing more than a very small amount of growth (this applies especially to daffodils and hyacinths). Choose plump, firm, well-rounded bulbs.

Watering

I have mentioned the subject of watering more times than some might think was necessary – but the importance of getting this right cannot be over-emphasized. Throughout mid-summer, make sure you check on your plants daily and water them as required.

← Repotting bulbs

Mid-summer is the time to repot those bulbous plants that flowered during late winter and spring. Remove the old bulb clumps, separate them and replant the healthy specimens into fresh compost.

LATE SUMMER

Plant bulbs outside

The majority of spring-flowering bulbs, with the exception of tulips, can be planted now. Textbooks often quote very specific depths for bulbs when they are planted. As a general rule, however, they should be planted so that there is as much soil above them as the height of the bulbs themselves. Exceptions are bluebells and daffodils, which should be planted twice their own depth. There are special graduated bulb-planting trowels available; these have a long narrow blade with measurements marked along the length of the blade, making it easier to determine the correct depth. It is important to ensure that the base of the bulb is in contact with the soil; air pockets result in the roots failing to develop.

Spring-flowering bulbs should be planted in autumn. Daffodils and other forms of *Narcissus* could be planted in late summer or beginning of autumn, as they produce roots early. The emerging young shoots of tulips can be damaged by winter frosts, so it is usually recommended that these bulbs are planted in late autumn – meaning that the young growth will appear after the worst of the winter weather.

↗ **Planter tool**
Bulb planters are inserted into the ground and when pulled out bring with them a plug of soil. The bulb is placed into the hole and then the plug of soil is replaced.

→ **Planting bulbs**
Planting bulbs outside is a job for late summer and early autumn. Generally the bulb should be planted at twice its own depth.

Tend to young and propagated plants

Those cuttings taken in spring should, by now, have grown roots and shoots and be independent plants. When you feel they are ready, they can be potted up and moved out into frames, or shady spots outdoors.

Plant up a sink or trough

This is a good time to plant up a container with alpines (see pages 56–59). The weather and soil will be warm enough so that the plants are nicely established before winter sets in. Water them well at planting time, but allow the container to dry at the surface before watering again.

> **ALPINE TIP**
>
> *Some people may be allergic to handling daffodils, tulips and hyacinth bulbs; they can cause a rash on the skin. Using gloves is generally more cumbersome, but it will reduce the risk, or the unwanted effects, of an allergic reaction.*

Sowing seeds

On page 80 we looked at the sowing of seeds in late winter, appropriate to some species. Others can be sown now. During late summer you can sow fresh seed (as soon as it has been harvested), of the following: *Anemone*, *Arabis*, *Campanula*, *Crocus*, *Dianthus*, *Narcissus*, *Primula*, *Pulsatilla* and *Saxifraga*. Collected seed can either be sown straight away or stored and sown later.

There are also several small biennial plants which, if not actually growing on the rock garden, will complement it if grown nearby, and these ought to have their seed sown now. They include forget-me-nots (*Myosotis arvensis*), wallflowers (*Erysimum*) and Canterbury bells (*Campanula media*).

EARLY AUTUMN

Clear leaves off rock gardens

It is important to remove dead and fallen leaves at this time of year. If they fall on lawns they will kill the grass, on paths they can become slippery, if they fall into drains or gutters they can cause a bad blockage, and if they fall on to flower borders – and rock gardens – they can smother plants, depleting them of light and air. If left in place too long, the plants will perish. Collect and bag the leaves, and leave them behind a shed for a couple of years. They will turn into wonderful leaf mould that can be used to great advantage elsewhere in the garden. Burn leaves if there was a severe problem of mildew, rust or black spot on border plants during the previous growing season.

Consult seed and plant catalogues

Seed lists from specialist alpine societies and groups, as well as the wider seed and plant catalogues from commercial suppliers are generally delivered in autumn, and this is a good time to sit down and plan ahead.

Once you have decided on the plants you would like to have the following year, do get your order for them placed quickly. Specialist societies may have only limited stocks of certain

← Autumn leaves
A thick layer of fallen autumn leaves draped over alpine plants can rapidly cause the death of the plants. Therefore it is important that all leaves are removed as soon as possible after they have fallen.

varieties, and the choicer items will be snapped up first. Commercial seed suppliers and plant nurseries also run out of stock, so the simple rule is that when you find something you want, order it without delay.

Control rampant plants

There are a number of plants frequently seen growing on rock gardens that, in all honesty, are better grown in large gardens well away from small, delicate-looking alpines. The two most troublesome plants in this regard, in my experience, are bugle (*Ajuga* spp) and snow-in-summer (*Cerastium tomentosum*). Both plants have wonderful, decorative foliage, but they

are thugs. If left, they will creep over a rock garden, smothering everything in their wake. So I recommend that, now, after the growing season has finished, you check these plants and trim them back so that other plants may have full exposure to winter light and air. You may even need to rip out whole swathes of these plants, and replant just one or two rooted pieces for next year's decoration.

← **Control spreading plants**

Rampant rockery plants, such as deep red bugle seen here, can quickly spread and will soon take over a whole rockery. Autumn is a good time to control such plants, so that the remaining alpines have full exposure to winter light and air.

MID-AUTUMN

Care for the water courses

Most owners of rock gardens with moving water – cascades, waterfalls and fountains – will have submersible pumps, and there is a school of thought which proclaims that these should not only be left in the water all year round, but that they should also be working, pumping round the water 24 hours a day, 365 days a year. During really cold weather the water movement, or 'agitation', that these pumps provide ensures that the pool leaves at least a small area free from ice.

If you 'opt out' of this and prefer to remove the pump and store it over winter, then now is the time to disconnect it. Clean it out as best you can, as well as the associated pipework. Surface pumps, in any case, will need to be so treated at this time.

Alpine house hygiene

After a growing season in the alpine house, there will be things you need to do, and now is the time to do them. Follow this cleansing routine, and incidences of pests and diseases over winter and over the next year will be far fewer:

1. If you have used paint-on shading, wash it off now. Alpines need bright light over the winter, so no permanent shading should be in place. In fact, even if you use netting or roller blind shading, you should still clean the glazing, inside and out.
2. Using hot, soapy water, with a dash of garden disinfectant to get rid of any lurking pathogens, wash down all of the struts and glazing bars.
3. Clear pots and bench tops of fallen flowers, leaves and other debris. Sweep the staging clean. If you have the time now to clean pots and tools, do so, otherwise this particular job can be left to late autumn (see page 96).
4. Remove clutter from under the staging, and the half-brick wall (if you have one). Tidy any stored material.
5. Sweep and wash the pathway.
6. Alpines are tough when it comes to winter cold, but they are delicate when it comes to contaminants and chemical sprays. If pests and diseases are present on plants, treat individual plants rather than blasting all of them with a blanket insecticide.

Continue to collect leaves

Continue to collect fallen leaves from the rock garden, as well as pond or water courses. The further we go into autumn, the greater the likelihood that ignored leaves will sink to the bottom of the water, so be prepared to delve into the depths with your net or, even better, your hand! Try not to disturb the mud too much; many creatures will be hibernating in it.

→ **Waterfall maintenance**
A waterfall, cascade or fountain will more than likely have a submersible pump to drive the water around the circuit. If you prefer to remove the pump for the winter period, and take the opportunity to clean it as well, then mid-autumn is a good time to do it.

LATE AUTUMN

Install wet weather- and frost-protection

Plants with hairy rosettes, such as forms of *Meconopsis*, or those with cup-shaped centres to the leaf rosettes, such as *Sempervivum* and many forms of *Sedum*, could do with an umbrella put in place over the winter. Prolonged wet soil and moisture on the leaves can cause rotting and fungal growths. But this umbrella should allow light through, otherwise the plants will suffer by being kept in the dark. Provide protection now.

Surround vulnerable plants with a ring of twigs, bracken or pine needles then lay a piece of glass, or better still a sheet of rigid transparent plastic, across the top. This cover should be large enough to cover the plant comfortably, but it should be some 2–4in (5–10cm) clear of its leaves. Also, it is best if the cover is supported at a slight angle, so that water runs off and away from the plant. Keep the sheet in place by placing a brick on top.

Clean pots and tools

Most gardeners accumulate dirty pots and seed trays, compost bags, dirty tools and so on. This is a good time of year to give everything a clean and a tidy. Wash pots and trays with warm soapy water, discard broken pots, used fertilizer boxes and compost sacks. Arrange pots and trays by sizes so that they can be accessed easily when you need them next spring. Clean tools with hot soapy water and wipe over metal parts with an oil rag afterwards to help prevent rust.

Finally do a stock-take. What items have you run out of – compost perhaps, or twine, or plastic plant labels? If you make a 'shopping list' now and add to it over the winter period, in early spring when things are a little busier you will have a ready list of things you can buy afresh.

Plan an alpine holiday for next year

This is a good time of year to plan holidays for the coming year, and one of the real joys of collecting alpine plants is going to see them in their natural habitats. The world has some marvellous alpine 'hotspots', and a visit to the travel agent will enable you to arrange travel to the countries concerned. But which ones?

The Alps, in particular, have a rich diversity of alpine habitats. Lauterbrunnen and Bernese Oberland are to be recommended as centres for alpine plant hunting, and here you will find such treasures as gentians and campanulas. The higher-growing alpines, such as *Androsace, Soldanella* and *Ranunculus*, can be found on the slopes of the Schilthorn. Switzerland, Italy and France are all worthwhile alpine destinations.

Further south are the Pyrenees, on the border of Spain and France, and here the climate is generally drier and warmer than the Alps. Forms of *Narcissus* and *Viola* are commonly seen in the Sierra Nevada, and into Portugal.

The Canadian Rockies, the Rocky Mountains of Central USA, and the Cascade Mountains of Washington State have decent roads, decent accommodation and, it has to be said, a decent diversity of wild flowers, including the Lady's slipper orchids (*Cypripedium calceolus pubescens*) and alpine forms of *Lilium*.

Further afield you can trek the Himalayas (particularly the Marsyandi Valley in Nepal), or the Drakensberg Mountains of South Africa, or the Kosciusko Mountains of Australia, or the New Zealand Alps … there is a seemingly endless list of possibilities, and I haven't even touched China, Japan, the South American Andes, Eastern Russian or Northern Europe.

↑ Winter cover

Many alpine plants, particularly rosette and hairy-leaved types, do not want to be subjected to prolonged winter wet, so late autumn is a good time to install some form of winter protection over them to keep off the worst of the winter rains. A single pane of glass supported on bricks can work or, if you have a large raised bed of alpines, as seen here, you will need to erect some form of larger protective structure.

08

A–Z DIRECTORY OF ALPINE PLANTS

Pots of pleasure

The common snowdrop (*Galanthus nivalis* AGM) can be identified by its medium-sized flowers and little green markings on the inner petals and is commonly found in pockets on rockeries, in alpine sinks and alpine houses. However, it is not a true alpine, as it came originally from the cool, damp woodlands of western Europe.

HOW TO USE THESE MAPS

Before investing time, effort and, of course, money on new alpine plant purchases, you first need to understand your geographical location and what this means to the plants in your care. It is important to understand temperatures and the cold tolerance of plants. For many years the standard used in America has been the Harvard University-derived 'hardiness zones'. This original zone map was that of the US, but it has been adapted for use in the UK and Europe. These useful maps enable gardeners to judge how their plants will grow and thrive, wherever they live in the world.

As we know, alpine plants are usually from cold, mountainous regions, sometimes from very high altitudes. So if you live in the plains and lowlands of England, or anywhere else in Europe or North America, these maps really help you to understand which plants will survive in your garden without help.

KEY TO MAPS

■	ZONE 1	below −50°F (−46°C)
■	ZONE 2	−50 to −40°F (−46 to −40°C)
■	ZONE 3	−40 to −30°F (−40 to −34.5°C)
■	ZONE 4	−30 to −20°F (−34 to −29°C)
■	ZONE 5	−20 to −10°F (−29 to −23°C)
■	ZONE 6	−10 to 0°F (−23 to −18°C)
■	ZONE 7	0 to 10°F (−18 to −12°C)
■	ZONE 8	10 to 20°F (−12 to −7°C)
■	ZONE 9	20 to 30°F (−7 to −1°C)
■	ZONE 10	30 to 40°F (−1 to 4°C)
■	ZONE 11	above 40°F (above 4°C)

Typical plant hardiness zones for Western Europe

Areas within the maps are colour-coded into 11 distinct zones. Plants mentioned in this part of the book will be given a zone reference from Z1 to Z11. Find your location on the maps, and you can then identify which zone your garden falls into. Do not forget to take into account that cities are warmer than rural locations, and that planting shelter-belts of trees or windbreaks, can dramatically improve conditions for plants.

Typical plant hardiness zones for North America and Canada

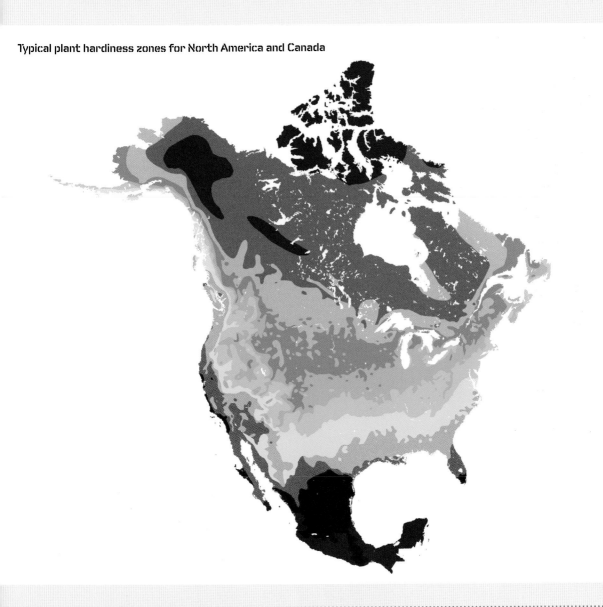

UNDERSTANDING THE PLANT INFORMATION

On the following pages I have selected nearly 90 of those alpine plants that have worked well for me over the years. Plants are listed alphabetically by their genus name and under each of the entries you will find these items of information:

ORIGIN: This tells you, if known, where the species was discovered. Understanding where a plant comes from – the country or part of the world, with its average climate or even altitude – can help you to understand its preferred growing requirements and conditions.

PLANT FAMILY: This is not something that is crucial for the average alpine gardener to know but it is interesting, nevertheless, to have a knowledge of which plants are related – botanically – to each other and to other plants you find in the garden. Some of the more important of the families covered in the following Directory include:
- *Alliaceae* (members of which include onions, leeks and garlic species)
- *Asteraceae* (the daisy, *Chrysanthemum*, *Dahlia* and *Aster* family)
- *Brassicaceae* (including vegetables such as cabbages and cauliflowers, but which also contains wallflowers, stocks and a host of other ornamental plants)
- *Crassulaceae* (a family of succulent plants, including *Sedum* and *Sempervivum*)
- *Cupressaceae* (a large family of coniferous trees and shrubs)
- *Ericaceae* (the family into which most of the acid-loving plants, such as heathers, rhododendrons and camellias fall)
- *Hyacinthaceae* (a family of bulbous plants that includes hyacinths, *Muscari* and *Ornithogalum*)
- *Iridaceae* (the huge *Iris* family)
- *Lamiaceae* (most herbs are included here, with mints, lavenders and sages)
- *Poaceae* (a family comprising many ornamental and cereal grass species)
- *Primulaceae* (members of which include primulas, *Cyclamen* and *Dodecatheon*)
- *Ranunculaceae* (the large buttercup and *Clematis* family)
- *Rosaceae* (the rose family also contains apples, pears, strawberries and *Potentilla*)
- *Saxifragaceae* (the large *Saxifraga* family also contains *Astilbe*, *Bergenia* and *Tiarella*)

TYPE: The 'type' of plant – for example, whether it is grown from a bulb as opposed to a tuber, corm or rhizome, or whether it is a mat-former, cushion-former or clump-former, or a sub-shrub, dwarf conifer and so on.

USDA ZONE: These are the climate zones referred to on pages 100–101, which were designed to identify the relative hardiness of plants. The zone numbers quoted here, based on UK Royal Horticultural Society data, is on the cautious side, so if you are not prepared to take any chances, follow the hardiness ratings to the letter. Otherwise there is a great deal of leeway. Raised beds, good drainage, sheltered gardens, and those with a sunny aspect, all give plants a better habitat – so be prepared to experiment.

MOST SUITED TO: This will give you some idea of which place in your garden is most suited to the plant. Usually this will be the rockery garden, but in some instances plants are better sited at the edges (for example, if they are rampant and need

← Edged leaves
Arabis alpina
subsp. *caucasica*
'Variegata' (see
page 108).

to be controlled), or within an alpine house (for example, if they are particularly small or need protection against the weather), or in containers, or in partial shade and so on.

DESCRIPTION: Here you will learn generalized details of the plant's shape, size and habit, along with flower and foliage colour and shape.

POPULAR SPECIES AND VARIETIES: Sometimes a plant species will exist without offspring or siblings. It will therefore have a relatively small entry in this book. But with, for example, the *Primula* genus, there are hundreds of species and cultivars (abbreviation of 'cultivated variety'), and so there will be many to recommend.

Award of Garden Merit

Throughout the directory section that follows, you will see the initials AGM set after certain plants. This denotes that the plant in question has passed certain assessments carried out by experts under the auspices of the Royal Horticultural Society in the UK. Only plants with exceptionally good garden qualities can be given this special Award of Garden Merit, and obtaining a plant with this distinction should give you a degree of guarantee and comfort. It is then up to you to make sure the plant you choose is appropriate to the situation, and then that you give it the love and care that it deserves.

Acantholimon ulicinum

Acorus gramineus 'Oborozuki'

ACANTHOLIMON

ORIGIN: Eastern Europe through Asia to Tibet
PLANT FAMILY: Plumbaginaceae
TYPE: Cushion-forming perennials
USDA ZONE: Z3
MOST SUITED TO: Alpine houses and landscaped beds

DESCRIPTION: Avid sun-lovers, plants in this genus relish hot, dry situations in perfectly drained soil. They will not tolerate winter wet. Most are spiny, hedgehog-like plants with flowers that are usually pink and surrounded by papery bracts. Do not disturb these plants once planted, and if grown in pots, repotting should be done with great care.

POPULAR SPECIES AND VARIETIES: All species of *Acantholimon* are alpine house plants, with the exception of *A. glumaceum* which can be grown outside. This species is a softer, less spiny plant than most in the genus, making a thrift-like cushion accompanied by sprays of pink flowers. Its similarity to thrift (*Armeria* spp) is not surprising as the two plants are related. *A. ulicinum* is a dense cushion plant with clusters of pale pink flowers held clear of the leaves, which form swathes of green that tumble over rock.

ACORUS (Sweet flag or sweet rush)

ORIGIN: North America, Asia, Europe
PLANT FAMILY: Acoraceae
TYPE: Grass-like perennials
USDA ZONE: Z4–5
MOST SUITED TO: Rock gardens in partial shade

DESCRIPTION: Technically this is neither a grass nor a bamboo, yet it has the appearance of both. It is actually a member of the *Arum* family. Its flowers, although not showy, are typical of the arum's 'spathes'. All forms of *Acorus* are usually found close to water, and the narrow, flat, grass-like leaves come from the root area in a distinct fan-shape, unlike any grass.

POPULAR SPECIES AND VARIETIES: There are three species generally available, but only one (*Acorus gramineus*), is of interest to rock gardeners. The plain green-type species is of little use in itself, so try the more attractive 'Variegatus' (green leaves with a central white stripe), 'Oborozuki' (yellow-gold leaves with slight green striping) and 'Ogon' (half-green, half-white). *A. gramineus* var. *pusillus* is a 2in (5cm) high tuft of grassy leaves and enjoys a slightly moister situation.

Aethionema 'Warley Rose' AGM

Ajuga reptans 'Variegata'

AETHIONEMA

ORIGIN: Europe, the Mediterranean region and south-west Asia
PLANT FAMILY: Brassicaceae
TYPE: Semi-shrubby perennials
USDA ZONE: Z7
MOST SUITED TO: Rock gardens in the open

DESCRIPTION: This is a genus of short-lived, evergreen or semi-evergreen perennials and sub-shrubs (and one or two that are distinctly shrub-like). They are grown for their prolific flowering from early summer onwards. Blooms are wallflower-like (they are related), and usually in shades of pink. Although lime-lovers, they will all tolerate neutral or even slightly acidic soils.

POPULAR SPECIES AND VARIETIES: *Aethionema grandiflorum* first came to the UK in 1879, from its native Lebanon and Iran. It makes a 12in (30cm) high bushlet of tangled, woody stems, and its flowers from late spring until late summer are of a delicious pink and white. The hybrid 'Warley Rose' AGM has tiny, linear bluish green leaves and flowers of bright pink appear in late spring and summer. 'Warley Ruber' is a slightly deeper pink.

AJUGA (Bugle)

ORIGIN: Europe, Middle East
PLANT FAMILY: Lamiaceae
TYPE: Creeping perennials
USDA ZONE: Z6
MOST SUITED TO: Rock garden edges

DESCRIPTION: Bugles are not alpine plants and they can be too rampant for most rockeries; however, when grown at the edges of a rock garden, and if strictly controlled by cutting back each year, they make useful plants with attractive foliage and short spikes of blue or pink flowers in early summer. They like a moist soil and will tolerate dappled shade.

POPULAR SPECIES AND VARIETIES: The most numerous members of this family in cultivation are varieties of *Ajuga reptans*, which produce flowers of royal blue over deep green leaves. The varieties have been bred for their rich leaf colourings, including 'Braunherz' AGM (purple bronze) and 'Burgundy Glow' (maroon and cream, and light blue flowers); both grow to 6in (15cm) or so in height. 'Catlin's Giant' AGM reaches 10in (25cm). The main feature of 'Variegata' is its brightly variegated leaves.

Allium flavum AGM

Allium karataviense AGM

ALLIUM (Ornamental onion)

ORIGIN: Throughout the Northern Hemisphere

PLANT FAMILY: Alliaceae

TYPE: Bulbous perennials

USDA ZONE: Z5–9

MOST SUITED TO: Sunny rock gardens and the alpine house

DESCRIPTION: Valued for their rounded heads of tubular flowers in shades of blue, purple, pink, white or yellow, alliums are perhaps more familiar as border plants. They have long leaves, which can be either thick or strap-shaped. Sometimes these leaves die down before the flowers appear. The *Allium* genus (to which vegetable onions, leeks and garlic belong) is vast, yet only a handful of species are valuable as alpine plants. The alpine forms like a gritty, but not poor soil, and must be planted in full sun.

POPULAR SPECIES AND VARIETIES: *Allium mairei* var. *amabile* is a rich, reddish purple-flowered alpine onion growing on a rhizomatous root rather than a bulb. It makes a delicate tuft of fine leaves and its flowers appear in late summer. *A. flavum* AGM has yellow flowers and must have a hot, dry spot. It grows to some 10in (25cm), but even smaller is *A. flavum* subsp. *flavum* var. *minus* at 8in (20cm) and which has straw-coloured flowers. *A. karataviense* AGM produces white flowerheads on sturdy 8in (20cm) high stems in mid- to late spring. *A. cyaneum* AGM has bright blue, star-shaped flowers in early summer. *A. sphaerocephalon* produces egg-shaped flowerheads of salmon pink and brick red. *A. moly* (known as golden garlic), with its golden yellow flowers, spreads rapidly. *A. insubricum* AGM is a beautiful 6in (15cm) high plant, hardly recognizable as an 'onion', with burgundy-coloured bells in mid- and late summer. *A. oreophilum* is a cheerful plant, the carmine flowers of which are umbrella-shaped and appear somewhat oversized for the plant. Look for the cultivar 'Zwanenburg', which is rich red.

Andromeda 'Compacta'

Androsace 'Millstream'

ANDROMEDA POLIFOLIA (Marsh andromeda)

ORIGIN: British native, distributed through central and northern Europe
PLANT FAMILY: Ericaceae
TYPE: Low, spreading evergreen shrubs
USDA ZONE: Z2
MOST SUITED TO: Rock gardens or peat beds

DESCRIPTION: Generally the andromedas are too tall for rock gardens, but *A. polifolia* provides a few fascinating miniature shrubs. It needs a lime-free soil and does not like being in full sun. It grows to a height of about 18in (45cm) and has woody stems clothed in small, hard, leathery leaves. The pink, bell-shaped flowers are carried in small clusters at the tips of the shoots.

POPULAR SPECIES AND VARIETIES: The more desirable forms for the rock garden include 'Compacta', which is smaller than the straight species, and 'Compacta Alba' with white flowers.

ANDROSACE

ORIGIN: Throughout Europe and Asia
PLANT FAMILY: Primulaceae
TYPE: Mat- or cushion-forming perennials
USDA ZONE: Z3–7
MOST SUITED TO: All grow in the alpine house; some will tolerate outdoor troughs or scree beds, but deserve winter protection.

DESCRIPTION: These are high mountain plants and possess real grace. Some produce neat cushions of narrow leaves, while others form a mat of woolly rosettes on strawberry-like stolons. The so-called aretian androsaces make perfect miniature domes of tiny, tightly packed rosettes with small, round flowers studding their surfaces.

POPULAR SPECIES AND VARIETIES: *Androsace alpina*, an aretian from the Alps, produces a cushion of green leaves, topped by rose-pink flowers. *A. vandellii* is one of the most beautiful of all alpines, with its tight, flattened domes of silver, and then, in good forms, hides them completely with round, white flowers. Also look out for 'Millstream' with lovely apple-blossom pink and white flowers.

Anemone ranunculoides AGM

Arabis 'Old Gold'

ANEMONE

ORIGIN: North America, Europe, Asia
PLANT FAMILY: Ranunculaceae
TYPE: Rhizomatous and tuberous perennials
USDA ZONE: Z4–8
MOST SUITED TO: The alpine house and well-drained rockeries in partial shade

DESCRIPTION: There are a great many species and cultivars of *Anemone*, ranging from 6in (15cm) to 4ft (1.2m) in height. There are a few that can be thought of as alpines, with flowers appearing from late winter until the middle of summer, depending on variety. These are easy plants, which grow best in cool positions and leafy soils.

POPULAR SPECIES AND VARIETIES: *Anemone blanda* AGM grows from tubers and is available in shades of white, pink and blue-purple. It has open, daisy-like flowers and is normally at its best in early spring. It grows to a height of just 6in (15cm). Those to look out for include 'Radar' AGM, a bright magenta, daisy-like bloom with a white centre, and 'White Splendour' AGM, with large, pure white flowers. The wood ginger (*A. ranunculoides* AGM) has toothed leaves and short, wiry stems carrying yellow flowers in early spring.

ARABIS

ORIGIN: Throughout the Northern Hemisphere and South America
PLANT FAMILY: Brassicaceae
TYPE: Hummock-forming sub-shrubs
USDA ZONE: Z2–7
MOST SUITED TO: Sunny walls and large rock gardens

DESCRIPTION: This is a genus consisting of a few very good alpine plants and a great many weeds. Generally these plants are easy to grow, provided they are planted in a sunny place. They are best grown in the same spots and require the same conditions as *Aubrieta* and *Aurinia*.

POPULAR SPECIES AND VARIETIES: The most frequently seen species, along with its many cultivars, is *Arabis alpina* subsp. *caucasica*. A variable plant, it carries white flowers, but you should also look for 'Schneehaube' AGM, an even better white, as well as 'Corfe Castle' (rosy red) and 'Rosea' (pink). 'Variegata' has white flowers and leaves edged with cream. *A. ferdinandi-coburgii* forms mats of grey-green leaves, which become green in winter. The form with the most dramatic leaf markings (deep cream with a central splash of green) is 'Old Gold'. White flowers are produced on short stems.

Armeria juniperifolia 'Bevan's Variety' AGM

Aubrieta deltoidea 'Doctor Mules' AGM

ARMERIA (Thrift or Sea pink)

ORIGIN: Throughout Europe, Siberia, Mongolia, North Africa and Alaska
PLANT FAMILY: Plumbaginaceae
TYPE: Tufted perennials
USDA ZONE: Z1–8
MOST SUITED TO: Open rock or scree gardens; good for coastal situations

DESCRIPTION: These are closely tufted plants, often forming dense cushions of very narrow, grass-like leaves. The flowers appear as papery globular heads, usually pink. Thrift has a definite coastal and maritime connotation, as it is frequently found on exposed beaches and headlands. It is therefore tolerant of high wind and salty air. In a garden situation these plants like sunny, gritty places.

POPULAR SPECIES AND VARIETIES: The most common form is *Armeria maritima*. It will be at its best in a poorish soil, where it can reach a height of some 6in (15cm). 'Alba' has white flowers. *A. juniperifolia* produces a tight bun of pink flowers on stems just 2in (5cm) high and is most at home in a sink or trough. Arguably the best cultivar is 'Bevan's Variety' AGM with rose-pink flowers.

AUBRIETA

ORIGIN: Europe to central Asia
PLANT FAMILY: Brassicaceae
TYPE: Low, trailing, evergreen herbs
USDA ZONE: Z5–8
MOST SUITED TO: Sunny walls and large rock gardens and screes

DESCRIPTION: These are hardy, evergreen, carpeting perennials, producing masses of very small, four-petalled flowers in shades of purple, mauve, blue, pink or white during spring. They are indispensable for rock or scree gardens and are arguably at their best on a low stone wall where they can hang over it. The small leaves are roughly oval.

POPULAR SPECIES AND VARIETIES: *Aubrieta* 'Doctor Mules' AGM is deep lilac, 'Red Carpet' is red purple and 'Aureovariegata' AGM has pale lavender flowers with green and cream variegated foliage.

Aurinia saxatilis AGM

Callirhoe involucrata

AURINIA SAXATILIS AGM (Rock garden alyssum)

ORIGIN: Central and south-east Europe
PLANT FAMILY: Brassicaceae
TYPE: Clump-forming and trailing perennial sub-shrubs
USDA ZONE: Z3
MOST SUITED TO: Sunny walls and large rock gardens

DESCRIPTION: The common rock garden alyssum is so-called because it used to be known botanically (and still by many gardeners today) as *Alyssum saxatile*. But as is so often the case, botanists change plant names for no good apparent reason and today this lovely plant sits alone in its own genus of *Aurinia*. The plant is often known as 'gold dust' because of the billowing heads of yellow flowers. It is best for bigger rock gardens as it can grow large and swamp rock and smaller plants in its wake. Fortunately it responds well to hard cutting back after flowering. In fact, this should be the annual routine, otherwise it becomes excessively woody. It combines well with forms of *Aubretia*.

POPULAR SPECIES AND VARIETIES: 'Compacta' is more dwarf than the species, 'Flore Pleno' has double flowers, 'Citrina' AGM is pale lemon yellow and 'Dudley Nevill' has flowers of orange-tan.

CALLIRHOE INVOLUCRATA (Purple poppy mallow)

ORIGIN: Central USA
PLANT FAMILY: Malvaceae
TYPE: Loose, spreading perennials
USDA ZONE: Z4
MOST SUITED TO: Landscaped alpine house; dry-climate, sunny rock gardens

DESCRIPTION: This is not a true alpine at all, but is frequently grown on rock gardens in the hottest, driest possible positions. It produces ground-hugging, far-spreading stems that are clad with deeply divided leaves. In late winter large cup-shaped flowers of brilliant crimson magenta appear.

POPULAR SPECIES AND VARIETIES: Only the straight species is generally available.

Calluna vulgaris 'Liebestraum'

Erica carnea 'King George'

CALLUNA and ERICA (Heather, Ling and Heath)

ORIGIN: North America, northern and western Europe to Siberia

PLANT FAMILY: Ericaceae

TYPE: Low-growing, ground-covering and clump-forming sub-shrubs and woody perennials

USDA ZONE: Z4

MOST SUITED TO: Rock gardens and containers

DESCRIPTION: Being accurate, heathers are forms of *Calluna*, whereas *Erica* is the genus of plants known as 'heaths'. However, they are generally grown together and only real enthusiasts are able to distinguish one from the other. Neither plant is what you would call a rock garden 'natural', yet they do frequently grow extremely well on rockeries, although they can look incongruous when next to true alpines. Both plants grow best in an acid soil. Callunas produce flowers in summer and early autumn. Many varieties have very attractive winter and early spring foliage, which can be as much a feature as the flowers. Choose the correct forms of *Erica* and you can have a succession of flower colour more or less all year round. Plants can vary in height from 3–18in (7.5–45cm).

POPULAR SPECIES AND VARIETIES: The best callunas are cultivars of *Calluna vulgaris*. Look for 'Liebestraum' (dark green foliage with amethyst-coloured flowers in late summer and early autumn), 'Golden Turret' (golden yellow foliage and white flowers) and 'Corbett's Red' (mid-green leaves and sugar pink flowers from late summer onwards). As for ericas, there are more than a hundred cultivars. Summer-flowering forms include *E. vagans* 'Mrs D.F. Maxwell' AGM (deep cerise flowers with dark brown stamens) and 'Valerie Proudley' AGM (white). If your soil is more alkaline than acid, then you will need to grow heathers in containers using an ericaceous compost, or grow *E. erigena*, a lime-tolerant winter-flowering species. Two excellent forms of this are 'Golden Lady' AGM (golden yellow leaves and white flowers) and 'W.T. Rackliff' AGM (dark green leaves and white flowers with brown stamens). Most of the winter-flowering types are forms of *Erica carnea*, and two to watch out for are 'King George' (dark green leaves and deep pink flowers from early winter to mid-spring) and 'Ruby Glow' (pale mauve flowers age to reddish purple, and are produced from mid-winter).

Campanula carpatica AGM

Cerastium tomentosum

CAMPANULA (Bellflower)

ORIGIN: Throughout the Northern Hemisphere; the alpine species mentioned below are European, seen around the Carpathian Mountains
PLANT FAMILY: Campanulaceae
TYPE: Forms for the rock garden are trailing, mat- and clump-forming perennials
USDA ZONE: Z3–8
MOST SUITED TO: Sunny rock gardens and screes

DESCRIPTION: This is a large genus of perennial and biennial plants, which could easily fill more than half this book. They are sun-loving plants, easily grown in any ordinary, good, gritty soil. They mostly flower in mid- and late summer.

POPULAR SPECIES AND VARIETIES: *Campanula arvatica* is a mat-former with leafy stems less than 3in (7.5cm) long. Its star-shaped summer flowers are bright violet blue. The tussock bellflower (*C. carpatica* AGM) is similar but is more of a trailer. Native to the Carpathian Mountains, the species itself is rare. Its hybrids in shades of blue, purple and white are better. *C. fragilis* is a low-grower at 6in (15cm) and from the Italian Alps. Open blue summer flowers are backed by clusters of green, serrated-edged leaves on woody stalks.

CERASTIUM (Mouse-ear chickweed)

ORIGIN: The mountains of Europe and western Asia
PLANT FAMILY: Caryophyllaceae
TYPE: Tufted, mat-forming and creeping perennials
USDA ZONE: Z3–4
MOST SUITED TO: Large, open, sunny rock gardens, screes and walls

DESCRIPTION: A group of many weeds and a few good rock garden plants, all are easily grown. Choose a sunny spot and a good soil. These are spring- and summer-flowering plants. Be warned, however – the so-called snow-in-summer (*Cerastium tomentosum*) is rampant and many who have planted it on a rock garden have regretted it, for it needs annual cutting back otherwise it will take over. In its favour, though, it will transform an area for many months with a carpet of beautiful, lush white flowers and silver foliage.

POPULAR SPECIES AND VARIETIES: Another useful species of *Cerastium* is *C. alpinum*, a mat-forming, grey-green plant useful for ground-cover; its white flowers covering the plant in late spring. *C. alpinum* var. *lanatum* has leaves that are more densely covered with grey hairs.

Chamaecyparis obtusa 'Nana' AGM

Chamaecyparis pisifera 'Nana'

CHAMAECYPARIS (False cypress)

ORIGIN: Eastern Asia, North America

PLANT FAMILY: Cupressaceae

TYPE: Evergreen coniferous trees and shrubs

USDA ZONE: Z5–8

MOST SUITED TO: Medium to large rock gardens in full sun

DESCRIPTION: Some species of *Chamaecyparis* can reach heights of 80ft (25m) and widths of 20ft (6m), so you would be forgiven for thinking that this genus is misplaced in this book. Fortunately there are many forms that are dwarf or slow growing, and can be grown on the open rock garden with relative confidence that they will not cause a problem. All forms have dense fronds of typical cypress conifer foliage and green, yellow and blue shades are available.

POPULAR SPECIES AND VARIETIES: Forms for the rock garden include *Chamaecyparis lawsoniana* 'Aurea Densa' AGM, one of the finest dwarf conifers for year-round colour as it has bright green-yellow foliage. For the first 10 years of its life it will reach just 18in (45cm), but ultimately it could grow to 8ft (2.5m). 'Green Glob' is a true miniature, discovered as a chance seedling in New Zealand. It slowly makes a dense cushion of rich green foliage that compels you to stroke it! It is good for troughs and sinks as well as the rock garden, as it reaches just 8in (20cm) in 10 years, with an ultimate height of just 18in (45cm). 'Gnome' is another good form and very similar, but less rounded and compact. 'Minima Glauca' AGM makes a broadly pyramidal bush, with fan-shaped sprays of bluish green foliage. It grows to just 24in (60cm) in 10 years, with an ultimate height of 10ft (3m). The Hinoki cypress (*C. obtusa*) – 'Kosteri' has twisted, lustrous foliage and is extremely slow growing, eventually reaching a height of 24in (60cm). *C. obtusa* 'Nana' AGM is very slow to form a flattened bun-shape of dark green foliage. *C. pisifera* is the Sawara cypress; one of the best forms for the rock garden, and a true miniature, is 'Nana', a compact conifer reaching 8in (20cm), with bright green foliage.

Chamaemelum nobile 'Treneague'

Chiastophyllum oppositifolium 'Frosted Jade'

CHAMAEMELUM (Chamomile)

ORIGIN: Western Europe and the Mediterranean region
PLANT FAMILY: Asteraceae
TYPE: Prostrate, soft perennial herbs
USDA ZONE: Z9–11
MOST SUITED TO: Growing between paving stones and at the base of a scree slope

DESCRIPTION: Chamomile has green, feathery foliage that has a wonderful, fruity, apple-like scent when crushed. Daisy-like flowers with cream-white petals appear in summer. They rarely grow to more than 6in (15cm). Although usually grown as ground-cover plants and even as lawn-substitutes, they thrive between paving stones.

POPULAR SPECIES AND VARIETIES: *Chamaemelum nobile* (which may still sometimes be found under its old name of *Anthemis nobilis*) produces flowers as described, but the variety 'Treneague' is non-flowering and so better for using as a lawn substitute. 'Flore Pleno' has double flowers.

CHIASTOPHYLLUM OPPOSITIFOLIUM AGM

ORIGIN: The Caucasus
PLANT FAMILY: Crassulaceae
TYPE: Tuft-forming, perennial succulents
USDA ZONE: Z7
MOST SUITED TO: Rock gardens, paving and containers

DESCRIPTION: These are crevice-loving plants, comprising tufts of apple-green rosettes of slightly succulent leaves. All summer long the bright yellow flowers come in long, hanging racemes, rather like open-work catkins. The plant grows to just 6in (15cm) or so in height and enjoys both full sun and partial shade. It is unusual to find a hardy alpine (other than *Sempervivum* and *Sedum*) in the plant family Crassulaceae.

POPULAR SPECIES AND VARIETIES: *Chiastophyllum oppositifolium* AGM is the only species to this genus. 'Frosted Jade' (sometimes this is sold as 'Jim's Pride') is a very attractive, variegated form.

Colchicum boissieri

Colchicum cupanii

COLCHICUM AUTUMNALE (Autumn crocus)

ORIGIN: Central and western Europe

PLANT FAMILY: Colchicaceae

TYPE: Perennial corms

USDA ZONE: Z5

MOST SUITED TO: Pockets on large rock gardens, scree beds, as well as in surrounding borders and the alpine house

DESCRIPTION: One of the most dramatic of autumn flowers, colchicums are crocus-like, and this confuses some people, especially bearing in mind the common name. However, these two plants are not related to each other at all. Colchicums arise, leafless, in late summer and early autumn and give a wonderful display of flowers. The leaves follow in late winter, long after the flowers have faded. When they are in full leaf colchicums are very large and can smother smaller plants. They are also poisonous.

POPULAR SPECIES AND VARIETIES: *Colchicum autumnale* produces masses of lilac-pink, goblet-shaped flowers – and all from a single corm. 'Alboplenum' is white, double and produces three to five flowers from each bulb. If you prefer something a little less showy, there is the single, white cultivar 'Album'. *C. speciosum* 'Atrorubens' is a vivid sugar pink, while 'Waterlily' AGM has purplish lilac double flowers. Another stunning species is *C. byzantinum*, arguably the most durable of them all. Each large corm can produce up to 20 crocus-like flowers of pale lilac-pink in late summer and early autumn. The flowers are just 4in (10cm) across, but watch out for the spring leaves which can be 16in (40cm) long and 4in (10cm) wide; they will smother nearby alpine plants if you are not careful. *C. cupanii* is pale pink with dark pink parallel veining; finally one of my favourites for growing in pots is the almost luminous purple *C. boissieri*.

Convolvulus lineatus

Cornus canadensis AGM

CONVOLVULUS (Bindweed)

ORIGIN: Southern Europe, Russia (Crimea),
North and South Africa, Asia Minor, and the US
(particularly Nebraska, Colorado, Texas and Arizona)
PLANT FAMILY: Convolvulaceae
TYPE: Climbing, scrambling and cushion-forming
perennials, annuals and shrubs
USDA ZONE: Z4–9
MOST SUITED TO: The alpine house and sunny rock
gardens, screes and walls

DESCRIPTION: This is a large genus of plants, the
most famous species of which is the familiar
bindweed, one of the most pernicious of weeds,
especially on a rock garden, where you may have
to dismantle the whole structure to eradicate
it. However, there are a few delightful forms of
Convolvulus for the alpine garden; all are avid
sun-lovers, and spring and summer flowering.

POPULAR SPECIES AND VARIETIES: *Convolvulus lineatus*
is a mat-forming plant with silver-green leaves
enhanced by funnel-shaped flowers in pink, blue
or white. *C. cneorum* AGM is a shrubby, non-
invasive plant, and is often seen in mixed borders.
It has silver leaves and white summer flowers,
and it needs a sunny, well-drained spot.

CORNUS (Dogwood)

ORIGIN: Temperate regions throughout
the Northern Hemisphere
PLANT FAMILY: Cornaceae
TYPE: Deciduous shrubs and deciduous
or evergreen trees
USDA ZONE: Z3–9
MOST SUITED TO: Large, sunny rock gardens

DESCRIPTION: This is a huge genus of shrubs and
trees, most needing a position in full sun in order
to thrive. They need careful siting so that they do
not swamp other plants. They thrive on heavy, wet
sites, but will grow on a range of soils, including
shallow chalk.

POPULAR SPECIES AND VARIETIES: *Cornus* 'Eddie's
White Wonder' AGM is a deciduous hybrid that
grows into a sizeable shrub. It has an upright
habit, and its dramatic rounded white bracts
are produced in mid-spring, covering the
branches. In autumn it has a further surprise
in that the foliage turns to bright orange.
C. canadensis AGM is known as the creeping
dogwood. Its low-growing foliage can be almost
hidden by the white flowers. *C. florida* makes
a large deciduous shrub or small tree.

Crepis incana AGM

Crocus 'Ard Schenk'

CREPIS (Hawk's beard)

ORIGIN: Throughout the Northern Hemisphere, but the alpine forms mentioned here are mainly from Europe, particularly the Alps

PLANT FAMILY: Compositae

TYPE: Clump-forming perennials

USDA ZONE: Z5–6

MOST SUITED TO: Rock gardens, screes or gravelly meadows

DESCRIPTION: Only two species of *Crepis*, both producing daisy-like flowers, are likely to tempt alpine gardeners. Both are sun-loving and flourish in any good garden soil.

POPULAR SPECIES AND VARIETIES: *Crepis incana* AGM comes from Greece and produces rosettes of narrow, grey (hairy) leaves. Stiff, branched stems, as much as 12in (30cm) high, carry masses of pink flowers over a long period in summer. The cultivar 'Pink Mist' is a paler pink. *C. aurea* carries tufts of dandelion-like leaves, with heads of orange flowers on short stems in summer.

CROCUS

ORIGIN: Central and southern Europe, Middle East, central Asia and northern Africa

PLANT FAMILY: Iridaceae

TYPE: Perennial corms

USDA ZONE: Z4–8

MOST SUITED TO: Rock gardens, beds, walls and screes in sun or partial shade, and the alpine house

DESCRIPTION: Crocuses are one of the true harbingers of spring and are among the best known and most popular of all the early blooming bulbous plants. Most forms are easy to grow, free flowering and increase well in suitable conditions. They are usually around 4in (10cm) or so in height. Despite flowering early, weak sunshine in mild weather will encourage them to open their flowers wide, making a very colourful show.

POPULAR SPECIES AND VARIETIES: There are more than 80 species, and while many can be grown in our gardens, those most likely to be found are cultivars. Generally sold as mixed colours, the Dutch crocus are arguably the best of the garden forms. You can still find plenty of named, single-colour cultivars to choose. (*Continued on page 118.*)

Crocus speciosus subsp. *xantholaimos*

Cyclamen graecum

CROCUS continued from page 117

They include the silvery lilac-blue 'Vanguard, the pure white 'Ard Schenk', the rich purple-violet 'Queen of the Blues' and 'Pickwick' with its striking purple striped blooms. *Crocus tommasinianus* AGM is one of the first to flower, in late winter and early spring. Its soft lavender flowers are small and slender. There are a number of varieties. Look for 'Whitwell Purple' (purplish-blue) and 'Ruby Giant' (deep purple). Crocus in the Chrysanthus group are free flowering. Growing to around 3in (7.5cm) in height, they are at their best from late winter to early spring depending on conditions. Look for 'Cream Beauty' AGM (soft cream-yellow), 'Snow Bunting' AGM (white), 'Blue Pearl' AGM (delicate blue with a bronze base and silvery blue on the outside of the petals) and 'E.P. Bowles' (clear yellow flowers, feathered with purple on the outside). *C. sieberi* subsp. *sublimis* 'Tricolor' AGM is very distinctive, with lilac blooms, each possessing a large yellow throat and broad white band. *C. kotschyanus* AGM comes into its own in early autumn, when its pale lilac, yellow-throated blooms appear. Finally, for late autumn: the saffron crocus (*C. sativus*) has large purple flowers with three deep red stigmas that are the source of the spice saffron; and *C. speciosus* subsp. *xantholaimos* has lovely, pale lilac flowers with deep purple veining.

CYCLAMEN

ORIGIN: Southern Europe and the Mediterranean region

PLANT FAMILY: Primulaceae

TYPE: Tuberous perennials

USDA ZONE: Z6–9

MOST SUITED TO: Rock gardens, beds, walls and screes in sun or partial shade, and the alpine house

DESCRIPTION: Although most people think of cyclamen as winter-flowering pot plants, the hardier (yet more delicate-looking) outdoor forms are both graceful and extremely useful plants for growing in shady spots under trees. Most are usually around 4in (10cm) or so in height. But you don't have to grow them under a tree; they make a colourful carpet in any small area, and they seem to positively thrive on dappled to heavy shade, and dryness at the roots.

Cyclamen purpurascens AGM

Daphne x napolitana AGM

POPULAR SPECIES AND VARIETIES: The types seen most often are forms of *Cyclamen coum* AGM, which is at its best from mid- to late winter. The pointed buds open to light or dark pink, or white. Most have rounded leaves with lovely silver and green patterning in the top and plain dark red on the underside. Although the plants themselves are tough, the leaves can be damaged by a severe frost. Very similar in appearance is *C. hederifolium* AGM, which flowers in late summer. The first flowers often appear just after rainfall and blooms always appear before the leaves. There are both pink and white forms. A great attraction of the plant is the varied shapes and the marbling, blotches and silvering of the leaves – none are the same. Some other *Cyclamen* suited to a small garden include *C. repandum* (beautiful, reddish-purple, turned-back petals in spring), *C. purpurascens* AGM (large, purple flowers in late summer), *C. cilicicum* AGM and *C. mirabile* (both are pink in autumn), *C. cilicium* f. *album* (white flowers in autumn) and *C. graecum* (the pink flowers of which are held well clear of the heavily marbled foliage).

DAPHNE

ORIGIN: Europe, North Africa, temperate Asia
PLANT FAMILY: Thymelaeaceae
TYPE: Deciduous and evergreen shrubs
USDA ZONE: Z4–8
MOST SUITED TO: Rock gardens and screes

DESCRIPTION: Woodland daphnes are agreeable enough to look at: there is certainly no perception of ugliness surrounding them. But this is not the main reason for growing them. It is their scent, wafting across the garden on a still winter's day, that is like no other. The thick matt green leaves and the small whitish or pink flowers, and often the red berries as well are all attractive.

POPULAR SPECIES AND VARIETIES: *Daphne odora* is a small, rounded, evergreen shrub with glossy, dark green leaves. Slightly hardier and more widely grown is *D. odora* 'Aureomarginata' AGM, with narrow, cream-yellow margins around the leaves. The star-shaped, mauve-purple flowers, carried in clusters, are wonderfully fragrant. *D. bholua* 'Jacqueline Postill' AGM has highly scented blooms of purple pink. *Daphne* x *napolitana* AGM is an evergreen, dense bush with narrow leaves and purple flowers in late spring.

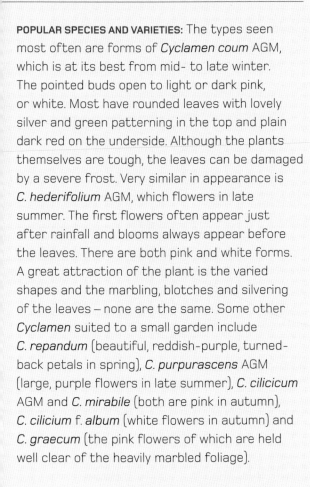

Delphinium nudicaule 'Laurin'

Dianthus deltoides AGM

DELPHINIUM

ORIGIN: The alpine species originate mainly from
Afghanistan, the Himalayas and China, with one
species from the US West Coast

PLANT FAMILY: Ranunculaceae

TYPE: The alpine species are generally loose,
clump-forming perennials

USDA ZONE: Z2–5

MOST SUITED TO: The alpine house or rock gardens

DESCRIPTION: There are several alpine forms
worthy of inclusion here. Most are dwarf with
the flowers well apart from one another, some
on quite long stalks. They will grow happily in
any good soil and an open, sunny position.

POPULAR SPECIES AND VARIETIES: *Delphinium
brunonianum* produces basal rosettes of foliage
and flower stems carrying open heads of large,
purplish-blue larkspur flowers. *D. grandiflorum* is
a light blue. Now difficult to find, but worth it if
you can, *D. muscosum* is just 5in (13cm) tall and
entirely covered in silky wool, including the big,
blue, widely open flowers. *D. nudicaule* is from
California and produces loose heads of red or
orange flowers on short stems, the most intense
colouring coming from the cultivar 'Laurin'.

DIANTHUS (Carnations and pinks)

ORIGIN: Throughout Europe and Asia

PLANT FAMILY: Caryophyllaceae

TYPE: Those most suited to the alpine garden
are tufted perennials

USDA ZONE: Z3

MOST SUITED TO: Containers, rock gardens, walls
and the alpine house

DESCRIPTION: *Dianthus* are at home in the border,
the rockery, containers and even as greenhouse
pot plants. All of the perennial forms are
evergreen (often with greyish leaves). Flower
colours range from white to deep mauve and
every shade of pink and red in between – there
are no oranges, yellows or blues. Sunny places in
good, gritty soils are best. Lime is not essential
but plants may be longer-lived in chalky soils.

POPULAR SPECIES AND VARIETIES: Try *Dianthus alpinus*
AGM with green (not grey) leaves and deep pink
or reddish flowers, and the cultivar 'Joan's Blood'
AGM with bronzed foliage and deep, blood-red
flowers with centres that are almost black.
The so-called maiden pink (*D. deltoides* AGM) is
extremely variable in its different forms, with very
dark green foliage and red or crimson flowers.

Dionysia curviflora

Dodecatheon meadia AGM

DIONYSIA

ORIGIN: Iran and Afghanistan
PLANT FAMILY: Primulaceae
TYPE: Tufted or cushion-forming sub-shrubs
USDA ZONE: Z3–5
MOST SUITED TO: The alpine house

DESCRIPTION: These plants are not ideal for the beginner and are not always easy to find. They can be tricky to keep. Damp, however slight, is usually fatal, otherwise they are perfectly hardy. Enthusiasts often grow *Dionysia* in double clay pots, with the space in between filled with pure sand – and only this should be watered. The compost in the pot should be gritty with very little loam added. These plants are astonishingly beautiful and are worth trying. All flower in spring and early summer.

POPULAR SPECIES AND VARIETIES: *Dionysia curviflora* grows in dense, compact huddles of rosettes of green or grey-green leaves and has many solitary pink flowers with a yellow eye. *D. aretioides* AGM is one of the less difficult species, and one of the most beautiful, with dense cushions topped by stemless yellow flowers. *D. bryoides* produces long-tubed, pink flowers.

DODECATHEON (Shooting stars)

ORIGIN: North America
PLANT FAMILY: Primulaceae
TYPE: Small, clump-forming perennials
USDA ZONE: Z3–8
MOST SUITED TO: The alpine house and sheltered rock gardens

DESCRIPTION: This is a genus of plants that enjoys the same conditions as the damp-loving primula family. In appearance they are something like primulas with long stems, at the top of which are cyclamen-like flowers – swept back petals in variations of pink and magenta, and also white. They flower in mid- and late spring.

POPULAR SPECIES AND VARIETIES: *Dodecatheon alpinum* has flowers of a reddish purple with a yellow tube and a purple ring on the throat. *D. pulchellum* subsp. *cusickii* has rich purple flowers with yellow throats. *D. dentatum* AGM is a striking plant with toothed leaves and lax heads of white flowers with dark anthers. *D. meadia* AGM is the best-known species and one of the tallest, with flowers on 2ft (60cm) stems. Masses of rose-pink flowers with white bases and reddish-yellow anthers are produced.

Epimedium grandiflorum 'Mount Kitadake'

Erigeron karvinskianus AGM

EPIMEDIUM (Bishop's mitre)

ORIGIN: Europe, North Africa, Middle East, China, Korea and Japan
PLANT FAMILY: Berberidaceae
TYPE: Clump-forming perennials
USDA ZONE: Z5–8
MOST SUITED TO: Rock and scree gardens in partial shade

DESCRIPTION: This is a genus of valuable plants that spread by means of creeping rhizomes. They grow in any reasonable soil and thrive in partial shade. They are handsome both in leaf and blooms, the latter appearing in spring, and are better enjoyed if the dead leaves are cut away before the flower stems grow too tall.

POPULAR SPECIES AND VARIETIES: *Epimedium alpinum* has open flowerheads comprising outer sepals of grey, speckled red – the inner ones being crimson, with yellow petals. *E. grandiflorum* AGM has flowers which are variable – they may be white, violet, deep rose pink or pale yellow. It will grow to 18in (45cm) in height if the conditions are good.

ERICA (see Calluna)

ERIGERON (Fleabane)

ORIGIN: North America
PLANT FAMILY: Asteraceae
TYPE: Mat- and clump-forming, and trailing perennials
USDA ZONE: Z4–7
MOST SUITED TO: Rock gardens, walls, landscaped alpine-house beds, paving and large containers

DESCRIPTION: Most varieties of *Erigeron* offered today are the result of hybridization. The genus, however, is largely ignored, which is a shame, as it is a large genus – of more than 150 species – comprising mainly perennials, but also annuals and biennials. All types are easy to grow, given a well-drained soil.

POPULAR SPECIES AND VARIETIES: The two most widely seen species are *Erigeron glaucus* and *E. karvinskianus* AGM. The former is a mat-forming, totally drought-resistant plant. It is also completely resistant to salt spray, which led to the breeding of the cultivar 'Sea Breeze', with bright pink flowers. *E. karvinskianus* is an excellent, near-prostrate plant for dry stone walls, rock gardens and crevices in paving.

Erinus alpinus var. *albus*

Eriogonum kennedyi var. *alpigenum*

ERINUS ALPINUS AGM (Alpine balsam)

ORIGIN: Western Europe

PLANT FAMILY: Scrophulariaceae

TYPE: Short-lived, clump-forming, semi-evergreen perennials

USDA ZONE: Z6

MOST SUITED TO: Rock gardens and walls

DESCRIPTION: These are pretty, tufted, tiny plants with pads of minute, toothed leaves and two-lipped flowers in lavender, pink, rosy mauve and white. They are never more than an inch or two in height. Flowers are carried from late spring to mid-summer.

POPULAR SPECIES AND VARIETIES: The best forms, which come true from seed, are 'Doktor Hähnle' (crimson), 'Mrs Charles Boyle' (pink) and *Erinus alpinus* var. *albus* (white).

ERIOGONUM (Wild buckwheat)

ORIGIN: Western North America

PLANT FAMILY: Polygonaceae

TYPE: Evergreen perennials and sub-shrubs

USDA ZONE: Z4–5

MOST SUITED TO: The alpine house

DESCRIPTION: This is a large genus of interesting and often beautiful plants, but which can be difficult to grow successfully. They are particularly intolerant of winter wet. You are most likely to have success with them by using very gritty, lime-free compost.

POPULAR SPECIES AND VARIETIES: *Eriogonum wrightii* var. *subscaposum* has grey, succulent-like foliage in loose rosettes; in summer, white or pink flowers with tight heads are held on stems 10in (25cm) high. *E. kennedyi* var. *alpigenum* is similar, with shorter, red-tinted flower stalks.

Erodium corsicum

Euonymus japonicus 'Microphyllus Aureovariegatus'

ERODIUM (Storksbill)

ORIGIN: Europe (particularly around the Mediterranean region) and Asia Minor
PLANT FAMILY: Geraniaceae
TYPE: Mat-forming and low, bushy perennials
USDA ZONE: Z6–9
MOST SUITED TO: Small rock gardens, sunny crevices or containers

DESCRIPTION: These plants are closely related to geraniums, but they are usually much smaller and have leaves divided or lobed along the midrib, rather than palmately from a central point. They like sunny, gritty, warm places with good drainage. They flower from spring onwards.

POPULAR SPECIES AND VARIETIES: *Erodium corsicum* has softly downy, greyish leaves and pink flowers with deeper veining. It resents winter wet. 'Album' is a white form. *E.* x *variabile* is, unsurprisingly, a variable plant. It is a cushion-forming and spreading perennial. Look for 'Bishop's Form' (pink lilac with maroon veins) and 'Flore Pleno' (possessing flowers that are double and pink).

EUONYMUS JAPONICUS

ORIGIN: China, Korea, Japan
PLANT FAMILY: Celastraceae
TYPE: Evergreen and deciduous shrubs and trees
USDA ZONE: Z7
MOST SUITED TO: Large rock gardens

DESCRIPTION: Although there are several forms of *Euonymus* (such as *E. fortunei* and *E. nanus*) that are more or less prostrate shrubs and are frequently planted on rock gardens, the forms most likely to be seen are the smaller *E. japonicus*.

POPULAR SPECIES AND VARIETIES: *Euonymus japonicus* has small leaves of green; much more interesting are the variegated forms such as 'Microphyllus Aureovariegatus' (with narrow leaves and yellow marking) and 'Microphyllus Albovariegatus' (green leaves with white edging). Keep bushes clipped to size. If you have the space on a rockery for something bigger you could try *E. fortunei* 'Emerald 'n' Gold' AGM (with green, gold and pink leaves), 'Emerald Gaiety' AGM (with green and cream leaves) and 'Silver Queen' (which has leaves with white edges).

Euphorbia myrsinites AGM

Festuca glauca 'Blaufuchs' AGM

EUPHORBIA MYRSINITES AGM (Spurge)

ORIGIN: Southern Europe
PLANT FAMILY: Euphorbiaceae
TYPE: Semi-succulent perennials
USDA ZONE: Z6
MOST SUITED TO: Walls and rock gardens

DESCRIPTION: Winding, trailing woody stems radiate from a central crown; branches are dressed with spirals of narrow, pointed, fleshy, grey-green leaves. During late spring and summer, the stems end in large heads of yellow bracts and flowers. It is seen at its best trailing over the face of a sunny wall or boulder.

POPULAR SPECIES AND VARIETIES: *Euphorbia polychroma* AGM produces its 'flowers' as bright, lemon-yellow bracts that cover the clumps of evergreen foliage for weeks in spring. It will reach a height of 18in (45cm). *E. characias* is an evergreen plant with upright, curved stems clothed in handsome, grey-green foliage. In early spring it produces yellow-green flowers with yellow spots at the centres, and will reach a height of 4ft (1.2m), so is best on top of a wall or at the back of a large rock garden.

FESTUCA (Fescue)

ORIGIN: Worldwide, but the forms best for alpine use originate from the European Alps and Pyrenees, as well as Greece and one species from New Zealand
PLANT FAMILY: Poaceae
TYPE: Tufted perennial grasses
USDA ZONE: Z5
MOST SUITED TO: Pockets on rock gardens and on walls, and the alpine house

DESCRIPTION: This is a large genus of annual and perennial grasses; a few of the latter are of use for tucking into crevices and odd corners on the rock garden. These grasses are grown principally for their thin, strap-shaped leaves; the flowers, which can sometimes be quite decorative, are seen usually during early summer.

POPULAR SPECIES AND VARIETIES: *Festuca alpina* produces 4in (10cm) high tufts of bright green foliage. *F. rubra* makes loose tufts of dark green, flat or rolled leaves that are up to 12in (30cm) tall. *F. glauca* (the blue fescue) has 18 or so cultivars, of which the best by far is 'Blaufuchs' AGM, with metallic-looking, silver-blue leaves.

Galanthus 'Magnet' AGM

Galanthus 'Merlin'

GALANTHUS NIVALIS AGM (Common snowdrop)

ORIGIN: Western Europe

PLANT FAMILY: Amaryllidaceae

TYPE: Bulbous perennials

USDA ZONE: Z4–6

MOST SUITED TO: The alpine house, containers, rock gardens, screes and wall tops

DESCRIPTION: Snowdrops are incredibly familiar; their nodding white flowers, make them one of our favourite winter-flowering bulbs. There are many species and cultivars, yet to the untrained eye they all look very similar. They have a large, almost cult following, with enthusiasts studying the minutiae of flower shape, colour, markings and so on. The common snowdrop (*Galanthus nivalis* AGM) is the most widely grown form. It produces its finest show in a fertile soil in partial shade. The blue-grey leaves are flat and strap-shaped while the white flowers have very small, green markings on the central sets of petals. Depending on varieties they can be 4–10in (10–25cm) in height.

POPULAR SPECIES AND VARIETIES: 'Magnet' AGM has heavy flowers that nod and move in even the slightest of winds; it is one of the biggest flowers. 'Flore Pleno' AGM is a double form, and among the named varieties look for 'S. Arnott' AGM, which is slightly scented and 'Viridapicis' with a green spot on both the inner and outer petals. 'Lady Elphinstone' has yellow markings. 'Straffan' is an old favourite with large blooms on 6in (15cm) high stems. 'Merlin' has green inner petals, and the whole flowerhead droops down very closely to the upright stem. *Galanthus elwesii* AGM is often called the giant snowdrop. Its broad, grey-blue leaves accompany the large flowers on 10in (25cm) high stems. The blooms have three long petals and three shorter ones with bright green markings. *G. ikariae* flowers in early spring; the wide foliage is bright, glossy green. This is a distinctive variety with long outer petals, the shorter inner ones have typical green markings.

Gentiana 'Strathmore' AGM

Gentiana verna

GENTIANA (Gentian)

ORIGIN: North America, Europe, eastern Asia, the Himalayas, New Zealand

PLANT FAMILY: Gentianaceae

TYPE: Upright or prostrate perennials

USDA ZONE: Z3–6

MOST SUITED TO: Rock gardens, containers and the alpine house

DESCRIPTION: With some 400 or more recorded species, the gentian is one of the most familiar plants for a rock garden. The characteristic blue of the trumpet-shaped gentian flower is legendary, but it is also possible to grow white, yellow, purple and red forms as well (these are primarily sun-lovers). Gentians have a reputation for being difficult to grow and even more difficult to flower but this is not true of all species. The cultural needs are too varied for a generalized statement, but it can be accepted that all the autumn-flowering Asian species and their hybrids are definitely acid-loving plants. They vary from 2–10in (5–25cm) in height.

POPULAR SPECIES AND VARIETIES: *Gentiana acaulis* AGM is easy to grow in any open, sunny situation and with good garden soil; but in some gardens it flowers readily, while in others it seldom does. Curiously, moving the plant, even a yard/metre or so from its current spot, may induce it to flower. *G. verna* is the popular spring gentian; a deep blue and certainly worth growing, but it is unfortunately not a very long-lived plant. *G. sino-ornata* AGM produces single blue flowers on creeping stems in autumn, while *G. makinoi* 'Marsha' produces them at the very tips of 24in (60cm) long stems in summer. The willow gentian (*G. asclepiadea*) has blue flowers in its leaf axils on arching stems, whilst *G. septemfida* keeps low, with tufts of blue trumpet flowers throughout summer and autumn. 'Strathmore' AGM is a hybrid with very clear, sky-blue flowers.

Geranium (Cinereum Group) 'Laurence Flatman'

Geum 'Borisii'

GERANIUM (Cranesbill)

ORIGIN: North-eastern Turkey

PLANT FAMILY: Geraniaceae

TYPE: Clump-forming perennials

USDA ZONE: Z6

MOST SUITED TO: Rock gardens, screes and wall tops

DESCRIPTION: Geraniums are perfect for sunny spots with only a couple of species tolerant of light shade. These are spring- and summer-flowering plants. You can often cut back the early forms to induce a second flush in later summer.

POPULAR SPECIES AND VARIETIES: *Geranium cinereum* originated in the Pyrenees and it is a true alpine of easy culture. Neat mounds of deeply cut grey-green leaves are carried on thin stalks, above which flutter cup-shaped flowers in deep pink, with deeper veining. The cultivar 'Laurence Flatman' is a favourite with a grounding of very pale pink and claret veining. *G. sanguineum* (known as the bloody cranesbill) forms a low mat of small, divided, rounded leaves, topped by large numbers of purple-magenta flowers over a long period. *G. sanguineum* var. *striatum* AGM has graceful, light pink petals veined with a deeper pink.

GEUM (Avens)

ORIGIN: Europe, Asia, New Zealand, North and South America, and Africa

PLANT FAMILY: Rosaceae

TYPE: Clump-forming perennials

USDA ZONE: Z3–6

MOST SUITED TO: Sunny rock and scree gardens, and wall tops

DESCRIPTION: Most geums are grown in borders, but a few are desirable rock-garden plants. They are spring or summer flowering, and require open, sunny positions in any good soil.

POPULAR SPECIES AND VARIETIES: The so-called alpine avens (*Geum montanum* AGM) has rounded, softly hairy leaves and rich yellow flowers on short, erect stems. The creeping avens (*G. reptans*) is one of the best, producing loose rosettes of leaves and rounded golden yellow flowers, followed by heads of seeds with long silvery tails. *Geum* 'Borisii' is a natural hybrid from *G. reptans* and from early to late summer it carries flowers of bright orange, centred with a boss of golden stamens, on 12in (30cm) high stalks.

Haberlea rhodopensis AGM

Hacquetia epipactis AGM

HABERLEA RHODOPENSIS AGM

ORIGIN: Eastern Europe
PLANT FAMILY: Gesneriaceae
TYPE: Rosette-forming perennials
USDA ZONE: Z7
MOST SUITED TO: Crevices in dappled to light shade

DESCRIPTION: *Haberlea* is a fairly small genus of diminutive evergreen perennial plants, grown for their elegant sprays of flowers. It is a useful rock garden or wall plant, but also likes a moist soil. It will flower in full sun, but produces a greater quantity of flowers if in dappled or light shade. *H. rhodopensis* AGM grows to just 4in (10cm) in height and has a spread of just 6in (15cm) or so. The leaves have a fine layer of soft hairs on both sides. Sprays of funnel-shaped, blue-violet flowers, each with a white throat, appear on long stems in late spring and early summer.

POPULAR SPECIES AND VARIETIES: *Haberlea rhodopensis* 'Virginalis' has flowers of pure white; *H. Ferdinandi-coburgii* is quite similar to *H. rhodopensis*, but the leaves are of a darker green and they are hairy on the underside only.

HACQUETIA EPIPACTIS AGM

ORIGIN: Eastern Alps
PLANT FAMILY: Apiaceae
TYPE: Clump-forming perennials
USDA ZONE: Z7
MOST SUITED TO: Moist rock gardens in partial shade

DESCRIPTION: Appears above ground as golden-yellow flowers surrounded by apple-green bracts. They are followed by the three-lobed, glossy foliage. Choose a peaty, moist, shady spot. It is valued for its very early flowering (in late winter and early spring). It grows to just 6in (15cm) in height.

POPULAR SPECIES AND VARIETIES: Normally only the species is found, but there is one cultivar, 'Thor' (sometimes listed by plant nurseries as 'Variegata'), which is similar to the species but has cream markings on the leaves.

Hebe x andersonii 'Andersonii Variegata'

Hebe 'Emerald Gem' AGM

HEBE

ORIGIN: New Zealand, Australia, South America

PLANT FAMILY: Scrophulariaceae

TYPE: Evergreen shrubs

USDA ZONE: Z6–9

MOST SUITED TO: Rock and scree gardens, large containers and landscaped beds in the alpine house

DESCRIPTION: Although hebes are fairly short-lived shrubs and vary considerably in their hardiness, they are incredibly popular – being grown for their flowers and their foliage in equal measure. The attractive flowers usually come in bottlebrush-like clusters at the ends of the shoots, each bloom comprising four petals joined at the base. Most natural or wild forms of *Hebe* have white flowers, but over the years breeders have bred into them shades of pink, blue, purple and red. The leaves come in two main forms: they are either the large-leaved types such as *Hebe andersonii*, and the cultivar 'Emerald Gem'; then there are the so-called 'whipcord' types, where the leaves are tight to the stems and scale-like, rather like a *Cupressus* (cypress) in appearance. Examples of this include *H. ochracea* 'James Stirling' AGM.

POPULAR SPECIES AND VARIETIES: For the general garden there are many dozens of forms from which to choose; the following are best on rock gardens. Of the whipcord types I would look for: *Hebe ochracea* 'James Stirling' AGM, with golden foliage and white flowers; *H. armstrongii*, with olive-green foliage and lovely white flowers; and *H. albicans*, a compact mound-former with bright green foliage and white flowers. All three reach 18in (45cm) or so in height. Some of the best of the large-leaved types for displaying their charms in a sunny spot are: *Hebe buchananii* (dark green leaves and white flowers); *H. pinguifolia* 'Pagei' AGM (the most often-seen *Hebe*, with blue-grey leaves and very dense spikes of white flowers; *H.* x *andersonii* 'Andersonii Variegata' (blue flowers, but the most dramatic aspect of the plants are the large, highly variegated leaves); 'Emerald Gem' AGM (emerald-green leaves and white summer flowers); and 'Youngii' AGM (dark green leaves on blue-black stems and violet blue flowers).

Helianthemum 'Rhodanthe Carneum' AGM

Hepatica nobilis var. *japonica*

HELIANTHEMUM (Sun rose or Rock rose)

ORIGIN: American continent, the Mediterranean region, North Africa, Asia

PLANT FAMILY: Cistaceae

TYPE: Evergreen shrubs and sub-shrubs

USDA ZONE: Z7

MOST SUITED TO: Rock gardens, pockets on walls or the front of borders

DESCRIPTION: Helianthemums are easy to grow, thriving in relatively poor conditions; they do, however, need a position in full sun (hence one of the common names). They are available in either single or double flower forms and the main colours are crimson, pink, flame-red, copper-orange, yellow and white. They grow to a height of 4–12in (10–30cm), and can spread to 24in (60cm).

POPULAR SPECIES AND VARIETIES: Look for the pale yellow 'Wisley Primrose' AGM or 'Rhodanthe Carneum' AGM with its rose-pink petals and central boss of golden stamens. The dozen or so excellent cultivars with the prefix 'Ben' include 'Ben Fahda' (bright yellow and leaves of grey-green), 'Ben Macdhui' (orange), 'Ben Nevis' (orange-yellow) and 'Ben Heckla' (copper-orange).

HEPATICA

ORIGIN: Europe, Asia, North America and Canada

PLANT FAMILY: Ranunculaceae

TYPE: Small, loose, clump-forming perennials

USDA ZONE: Z4–5

MOST SUITED TO: Rock gardens in part shade

DESCRIPTION: Hepaticas are related to anemones but are quickly distinguishable from them. The flowers are made up of coloured sepals with leafy bracts beneath. From resting buds, wiry flowering stems unfurl early in the year and are followed by the leaves, which are silvery and hairy when young. The flowers of the species are single and the usual colour is blue or mauve.

POPULAR SPECIES AND VARIETIES: *Hepatica nobilis* AGM is a herald of spring. From its tufts of three-lobed leaves come short stems, each carrying one shapely clear blue flower. There are dozens of variations on a theme, with white or pink flowers, some fully double. My favourite is, without doubt, *H. nobilis* var. *japonica* with white, pink and magenta flowers. *H. transsilvanica* AGM is rather similar to *H. nobilis* but slightly larger in all its parts.

Hypericum olympicum AGM

Iberis saxatilis

HYPERICUM (St John's wort)

ORIGIN: South-east Europe
PLANT FAMILY: Clusiaceae
TYPE: Evergreen shrubs
USDA ZONE: Z6
MOST SUITED TO: Open rock gardens and screes

DESCRIPTION: Hypericums are good in dry soil under walls and in part shade. With their five-petalled flowers of golden yellow and prominent stamens, they are easy-to-grow, undemanding shrubs. However, the most often seen species, *Hypericum calycinum* (also known as the rose of Sharon) is a thug and is not recommended for the rock garden.

POPULAR SPECIES AND VARIETIES: *Hypericum olympicum* AGM makes a low mounded shrub with erect stems densely clothed with small pointed leaves and rich golden-yellow flowers. *H. balearicum* is an evergreen, compact shrub growing to a height and spread of 24in (60cm). From early summer it produces solitary, large, fragrant blooms of golden yellow. *H. coris* is even better for the rock garden with a height of just 12in (30cm) and a spread of 8in (20cm). Its summer flowers come in heads of cup-shaped, bright yellow flowers each with red streaks.

IBERIS (Perennial candytuft)

ORIGIN: Southern Europe and western Asia
PLANT FAMILY: Brassicaceae
TYPE: Clump-forming sub-shrubs
USDA ZONE: Z6–7
MOST SUITED TO: Open rock gardens and walls

DESCRIPTION: Being a member of the Brassicaceae plant family the flowers have four petals, but in the case of *Iberis* these comprise two short petals and two longer ones. All plants in the genus (including the annual candytufts) are sun-loving. They are also easy-to-grow plants and flower in spring or summer.

POPULAR SPECIES AND VARIETIES: Various forms of the species *Iberis sempervirens* are the most popular and widely grown members of the genus. Look for cultivars such as 'Snowflake' AGM, offering pure white flowers in abundance. *I. saxatilis* is a neat little sub-shrub seldom exceeding 6in (15cm) with masses of white flowers, sometimes tinged with purple.

Iris reticulata 'Pauline'

Jeffersonia dubia

IRIS (BULBOUS)

ORIGIN: Temperate regions of the Northern Hemisphere
PLANT FAMILY: Iridaceae
TYPE: Dwarf bulbs
USDA ZONE: Z5–10
MOST SUITED TO: Pockets on open rock gardens, wall tops, containers and the alpine house

DESCRIPTION: This is an enormous genus, but we are concerned only with the dwarf bulbous irises, of which only a handful are regularly grown by alpine gardeners. The more familiar species include *Iris danfordiae* and *I. reticulata*. The first of them will bloom in late winter and early spring, especially if the winter is mild.

POPULAR SPECIES AND VARIETIES: *Iris danfordiae* has lovely, deep yellow flowers with green spots in the throat. *I. histrioides* 'Major' AGM has rich blue flowers just 6in (15cm) high. *I. reticulata* AGM has deep mauve flowers with gold markings. Named varieties include 'Harmony' (sky blue and royal blue, with yellow-rimmed white blotches), 'Pauline' (dusky violet-pink highlighted by a large white spot on the falls) and 'Katherine Hodgkin' AGM (large, pale blue flowers with yellow markings).

JEFFERSONIA

ORIGIN: North America and Asia
PLANT FAMILY: Berberidaceae
TYPE: Deciduous woodland perennials
USDA ZONE: Z5
MOST SUITED TO: The alpine house and shaded, moist, leafy rock gardens

DESCRIPTION: An uncommon genus, it was named in honour of Thomas Jefferson, President of the United States from 1801 to 1809. He had a deep interest in horticulture and was a patron of Botany. There are just two species available.

POPULAR SPECIES AND VARIETIES: *Jeffersonia dubia* has rounded, lobed, glaucous leaves sometimes tinted with violet on thin, wiry stems. Its spring flowers are solitary, cup-shaped and clear blue. Choose a gritty, but humus-rich soil in the open or in the alpine house. *J. diphylla* is a North American species with grey-green leaves deeply divided into two lobes. White flowers are carried on 9in (23cm) stems in early spring. This plant prefers a woodland soil in light shade.

Juniperus communis 'Compressa' AGM

Lachenalia aloides var. *quadricolor* (Darling)

JUNIPERUS COMMUNIS (Common juniper)

ORIGIN: Throughout the Northern Hemisphere
PLANT FAMILY: Cupressaceae
TYPE: Conifer
USDA ZONE: Z2–7
MOST SUITED TO: Large rock gardens, medium to large sinks and troughs

DESCRIPTION: Many junipers are natives to chalk soils and will nearly always perform well on alkaline soil – providing it does not get waterlogged or bone dry in summer. There are 60 or so species, but only a few are suited to rock gardens and rockery containers. Most prefer sunny positions.

POPULAR SPECIES AND VARIETIES: The Noah's Ark juniper (*Juniperus communis* 'Compressa' AGM) forms a tightly compressed miniature column of light green. *J. communis* 'Miniatur' has a softer green foliage, while 'Brynhyfryd Gold' has new spring foliage that turns to a soft gold colour. 'Green Carpet' spreads for 3–4ft (90–120cm) after 10 years, while only reaching a height of just 4in (10cm). *J. horizontalis* 'Blue Pygmy' is a true miniature, making a tiny clump of blue-green, more silvery in summer. After 10 years it is just 8in (20cm) high and wide.

LACHENALIA ALOIDES (Leopard lily)

ORIGIN: South Africa
PLANT FAMILY: Hyacinthaceae
TYPE: Bulbous perennials
USDA ZONE: Z9
MOST SUITED TO: The alpine house

DESCRIPTION: This bulb produces stems to about 12in (30cm) in height and it is found in the wild, southern parts of South Africa. Leaves are fleshy and strap-shaped, bright green flecked with purplish blue. The cigar-shaped flowers (carried on spikes arising from the centre of the plant) are red and yellow, faintly tipped green. They appear in late spring and early summer. These plants need rich, open soil and a bright sunny spot; definitely best in the alpine house.

POPULAR SPECIES AND VARIETIES: *Lachenalia aloides* var. *quadricolor* AGM has more intense colourings. *L. contaminata* AGM is smaller, with thinner, sword-like leaves and white flowers. *L. viridiflora* has curious, turquoise flowers.

Leontopodium kamtschaticum

Leptinella squalida 'Platt's Black'

LEONTOPODIUM ALPINUM (Edelweiss)

ORIGIN: The mountains of Eurasia, the Andes
PLANT FAMILY: Asteraceae
TYPE: Clump-forming, sometimes erect, branching perennials
USDA ZONE: Z4–7
MOST SUITED TO: Open rock gardens and the alpine house

DESCRIPTION: This genus includes the true edelweiss (*Leontopodium alpinum*) with its grey leaves and curiously attractive, white, daisy-like flowers. Although easy to grow, they are seldom long-lived plants. They come from the European Alps and are variable plants, particularly in lowland gardens. The grey-green leaves are not as well known as the white, felted flowerheads that appear in late spring and early summer. To me they always seem to look a little grubby.

POPULAR SPECIES AND VARIETIES: *Leontopodium souliei* is longer lived but not quite so conspicuous in flower. *L. kamtschaticum* has slightly larger leaves than *L. alpinum*.

LEPTINELLA

ORIGIN: Australasia and South America
PLANT FAMILY: Asteraceae
TYPE: Creeping perennials
USDA ZONE: Z5–8
MOST SUITED TO: Crevices in paving and rock gardens, as well as wall tops and sides, screes and gravel gardens

DESCRIPTION: These plants are grown for their neat, low carpets of fine, soft, often fern-like foliage. They are suited to planting in paving for they can withstand light treading (rather like chamomile, see page 114). They also make good cover for early spring bulbs. The *Leptinella*, is arguably at its best at the foot of the rock garden where its invasive tendencies can be controlled.

POPULAR SPECIES AND VARIETIES: *Leptinella atrata* is an evergreen mat-former with small, finely cut, greyish-green leaves and blackish-red flowers in late spring and early summer. *L. atrata* subsp. *luteola* is similar, but the flowers are enhanced by creamy-yellow stamens. Probably the easiest to find and grow successfully is *L. squalida* 'Platt's Black', with brown and black tints to the foliage.

Lewisia cotyledon Ashwood strain

Linum narbonense

LEWISIA

ORIGIN: North America and Canada
PLANT FAMILY: Portulacaceae
TYPE: Rosette-forming perennials
USDA ZONE: Z3–7
MOST SUITED TO: Sides of rockery walls, in crevices and in the alpine house

DESCRIPTION: These are among the showiest of alpines – and they can also be some of the most difficult. They are really only at their best when growing in a crevice in a wall, as they do not like wet conditions, and if moisture sits around the neck of the plant for more than a short period of time, it will rot.

POPULAR SPECIES AND VARIETIES: The great majority of lewisias are grown under the name *Lewisia cotyledon* AGM. Because propagation tends to be by seed, and these plants hybridize so readily, several species have effectively subsumed into one large species of cultivation. From the rosettes of fleshy leaves emerge multi-branched stems in late spring and early summer. These carry flowers in rose-pink, orange, peach, yellow and white shades, often with prominent veins.

LINUM (Flax)

ORIGIN: Throughout the Northern Hemisphere
PLANT FAMILY: Linaceae
TYPE: Clump-forming perennials, often with a woody base
USDA ZONE: Z5–8
MOST SUITED TO: Sunny rock gardens or screes

DESCRIPTION: This is the genus that contains the true flax. These sun-loving plants vary considerably, with centrally arising stems with conspicuous flowers in bright yellow, blue, pink and white, from late spring to mid-summer. They are best in dry soil and certainly dislike winter wet.

POPULAR SPECIES AND VARIETIES: *Linum arboreum* AGM is a shrubby form with grey-green leaves and clusters of large, deep yellow flowers. 'Gemmell's Hybrid' AGM is more compact and leafy and is very floriferous. The golden flax (*L. flavum*) needs to be in the alpine house as it is not entirely hardy. *L. narbonense* produces azure blue flowers at the ends of the stems, looking its best in early summer.

Lithodora 'Heavenly Blue'

Massonia echinata

LITHODORA

ORIGIN: France, south-west Europe

PLANT FAMILY: Boraginaceae

TYPE: Evergreen sub-shrubs

USDA ZONE: Z7

MOST SUITED TO: Rock gardens, low walls and the fronts of borders

DESCRIPTION: Low-growing (prostrate), evergreen hardy plants producing a shock of gentian-blue flowers are a rare thing in the garden, which makes *Lithodora* a valuable commodity. They need a sunny, moist but well-drained soil and generally prefer a neutral to acid soil. They do not reach much higher than 6–9in (15–23cm), but can spread a little further. Plants may still be found under the old name of *Lithospermum*.

POPULAR SPECIES AND VARIETIES: 'Heavenly Blue' AGM has trailing stems covered in small hairs and produces masses of deep blue flowers in summer. 'Grace Ward' AGM is similar but has a spread of just 12in (30cm).

MASSONIA

ORIGIN: South Africa

PLANT FAMILY: Hyacinthaceae

TYPE: Prostrate, bulbous perennials

USDA ZONE: Z9

MOST SUITED TO: The alpine house

DESCRIPTION: These are fascinating bulbous plants, found growing wild in very dry, sandy areas of Cape Province, South Africa. Plants have two opposite leaves, invariably lying on the ground. They may be smooth, veined or ridged and can grow to 5in (12.5cm) or so in length. Flowers appear in early summer, taking the form of dense, white clusters emerging from between the leaves; a mass of stamens protrude. Plants need a sunny spot – certainly best in the alpine house – and a very well-drained, sandy soil enriched with a little humus.

POPULAR SPECIES AND VARIETIES: *Massonia echinata* has deep blue-green, slightly ridged leaves and yellow-white flowers; *M. pustulata* is similar but with masses of small blisters to the leaves.

Narcissus cantabricus

Narcissus romieuxii var. romieuxii

NARCISSUS (Daffodil)

ORIGIN: Southern Europe, northern Africa, western Asia, China, Japan

PLANT FAMILY: Amaryllidaceae

TYPE: Bulbous perennials

USDA ZONE: Z4–6

MOST SUITED TO: The alpine house, pockets on the rock garden, and in sinks, troughs and other containers

DESCRIPTION: Ask anyone to name some 'spring flowers' and most will come up with the daffodil within the first two or three suggestions. Few plants epitomize more the essence of spring – and the promise of warmer days ahead – than the daffodil. They are the hybrid forms of large and trumpet-flowered narcissus, but here we are more concerned with the miniature species and hybrids, best suited to the alpine house and pockets on the rock garden. Choose an open, sunny spot, preferably sheltered from the strongest winds as these blast the flowerheads and cause them to be short-lived.

POPULAR SPECIES AND VARIETIES: There are hundreds I could recommend; in fact there are well over 1,200 species of *Narcissus*. However, my favourites (in no particular order) are: 'Rip Van Winkle', a double yellow, dwarf variety (some liken it to a loose dahlia flower), 5in (13cm) high; 'February Gold', golden yellow and early, one of the all-time best, 12in (30cm) high; 'Tete-a-Tete', golden yellow, multi-headed, long-lasting and dwarf, one of the best for garden or pots, 6in (15cm) high; and *Narcissus bulbocodium*, the hoop petticoat daffodil, golden yellow flowers with conical cups and narrow, pointed petals, 3–6in (7.5–15cm) high. *N. romieuxii* subsp. *romieuxii* is, by name a bit of a mouthful, but by appearance is delightful, with its paper-thin pale lemon-yellow trumpets, 6–8in (15–20cm) high. *N. cantabricus* is very similar but with near white blooms.

Nierembergia repens

Oenothera caespitosa

NIEREMBERGIA REPENS

ORIGIN: Argentina, Uruguay and Chile
PLANT FAMILY: Solanaceae
TYPE: Mat-forming perennials
USDA ZONE: Z7–8
MOST SUITED TO: The alpine house

DESCRIPTION: Leaves appear almost at soil level, and in fact this plant produces a number of stems that actually grow under the soil. The brilliant white, cup-shaped flowers are a little more than 1in (2.5cm) wide, borne in summer on very short stalks, just overtopping the dull green leaves. It is best kept in an alpine house, in a sunny position and in well-drained soil.

POPULAR SPECIES AND VARIETIES: Normally only the species is found (and it may be sold under its old name of *Nierembergia rivularis*).

OENOTHERA (Evening primrose)

ORIGIN: North America
PLANT FAMILY: Onagraceae
TYPE: Loose, upright perennials
USDA ZONE: Z4–7
MOST SUITED TO: Borders, rock gardens and wall tops

DESCRIPTION: The evening primroses vary in height, but I am including here only the shorter forms. They are mostly yellow-flowered, although white and pink forms are available. All have large, cup-shaped blooms. They are easily grown in sunny, well-drained positions.

POPULAR SPECIES AND VARIETIES: *Oenothera macrocarpa* AGM (formerly *O. missouriensis*) is unbeatable as a yellow-flowered perennial for the front of a border or base of a rock garden. Prostrate stems carry a long succession of large, wide open, lemon-yellow blooms, shown off by red calyces. It grows to less than 12in (30cm) and blooms through summer and autumn. *O. caespitosa* has neat, clumpy growth with large, white flowers on short stems, while *O. speciosa* has pale pink flowers with white and yellow centres. *O. fruticosa* 'Fireworks' AGM (sometimes known as 'Fyrverkeri') is yellow and free flowering.

Origanum vulgare 'Aureum' AGM

Oxalis melanosticta

ORIGANUM

ORIGIN: Asia Minor

PLANT FAMILY: Lamiaceae

TYPE: Sub-shrub or herbaceous perennials

USDA ZONE: Z5–9

MOST SUITED TO: The alpine house, containers or pockets on sunny, sheltered rock gardens

DESCRIPTION: These plants are distinctive for having catmint- or shrimp plant-like flowers in late summer. They need a well-drained soil and resent winter wet. The most famous is the herb marjoram or oregano (*Origanum majorana*), but the forms mentioned below are all better suited to rock gardens or alpine houses.

POPULAR SPECIES AND VARIETIES: *Origanum* x *hybridinum* has woolly, grey-green leaves from a compact root and wiry sprays carrying rose-purple flowers in summer. *O. dictamnus* is the Dittany of Crete that seventeenth-century army surgeons used to carry to treat wounds. It is not hardy, but has lovely greenish-pink, hop-like flower heads. *O. calcaratum* is similar but with mauve-pink heads. *O. vulgare* 'Aureum' AGM is a particularly good form of the wild marjoram, with golden leaves.

OXALIS (Sorrel or Shamrock)

ORIGIN: South America and South Africa, although has now naturalized worldwide

PLANT FAMILY: Oxalidaceae

TYPE: Mostly tuberous-rooted perennials

USDA ZONE: Z3–9

MOST SUITED TO: The alpine house, large rock gardens and nearby part-shaded borders

DESCRIPTION: This is a genus that includes two or three troublesome weeds, as well as many more good garden plants. They generally come from small, round tubers and several have the propensity to grow into large clumps if left to their own devices. Most have shamrock-like, tri-lobed foliage and small five-petalled, trumpet-like flowers.

POPULAR SPECIES AND VARIETIES: *Oxalis melanosticta* (USDA Z9) has soft, fine-haired leaves and bright, golden yellow flowers. Arguably not for the rock garden, but a part-shady spot nearby, *O. acetosella* (USDA Z3) is the wood sorrel with white flowers; *O. acetosella* var. *rosea* has pink flowers. These plants can spread very rapidly. *O. laciniata* is one of the finest of all alpines, with deep royal-purple flowers that open up from tightly wound rolls.

Penstemon hirsutus var. *pygmaea*

Phlox divaricata subsp. *laphamii* 'Chattahoochee' AGM

PENSTEMON (Beard tongue)

ORIGIN: North and central America

PLANT FAMILY: Scrophulariaceae

TYPE: Clump-forming perennials

USDA ZONE: Z6–8

MOST SUITED TO: The alpine house, open sunny rock gardens and screes, and wall tops

DESCRIPTION: Herbaceous penstemons derive from several species. These plants are hardy everywhere, but they may be cut annually to the ground by frosts in cold districts (elsewhere they are evergreen). As a general rule the larger the leaves and flowers, the less hardy the variety.

POPULAR SPECIES AND VARIETIES: *Penstemon pinifolius* AGM grows erectly with narrow leaves and sprays of scarlet flowers on 8in (20cm) high stems. 'Mersea Yellow' is a pleasing variation with golden-yellow flowers. *P. laetus* subsp. *roezlii* is low growing at 6in (15cm) with deep red flowers. *P. hirsutus* var. *pygmaeus* has reddish leaves and showy tubular flowers of lilac-pink in early to mid-summer.

PHLOX

ORIGIN: North America

PLANT FAMILY: Polemoniaceae

TYPE: The alpine forms are mound- and mat-forming perennials

USDA ZONE: Z3–6

MOST SUITED TO: Rock gardens, screes, the alpine house, sinks, troughs and raised beds

DESCRIPTION: There are very small perennial phloxes and there are some very large ones (and there are some decorative annuals types as well). For the alpine enthusiast, however, there are a dozen or so species, sporting hundreds of cultivars. They are mostly happy in a well-drained soil in sun.

POPULAR SPECIES AND VARIETIES: *Phlox subulata* is an evergreen, mound-forming perennial just 4in (10cm) high and with a spread of twice this. Masses of star-shaped white, pink or mauve flowers appear in early summer. *P. douglasii* is a prickly species with mauve flowers. Look for the cultivars 'Apollo', 'Boothman's Variety' AGM, 'Crackerjack' AGM, and 'Iceberg' AGM. *P. divaricata* subsp. *laphamii* 'Chattahoochee' AGM is not mat-forming, but makes a loose tangle of stems, to a height of just 6–8in (15–20cm) or so.

Picea abies 'Elegans'

Pleione (mixed hybrids)

PICEA (Spruce)

ORIGIN: Most of the Northern Hemisphere
(except Africa)
PLANT FAMILY: Pinaceae
TYPE: Evergreen conifers
USDA ZONE: Z3–4
MOST SUITED TO: Large rock gardens

DESCRIPTION: The spruces are narrow-crowned
evergreen trees. They generally have strong main
stems, with little side-branching. Many will grow
to large trees of parkland dimensions, but there
are a few dwarfs for the rock garden.

POPULAR SPECIES AND VARIETIES: *Picea pungens*
Glauca Group 'Glauca Prostrata' is a conifer
with a prostrate (or 'procumbent') habit that is
undeniably attractive in a rock-garden setting.
The beautiful bluish needles clothe the branches.
There are occasions when upright shoots may
develop, and these should be snipped off with
secateurs, otherwise they may take over and
change the habit of the plant and make it too big
for a rockery situation. *P. abies* 'Elegans' is hard to
find but worth the search. It makes a deep green
mound and is a dwarf, not a miniature.

PLEIONE (Indian crocus)

ORIGIN: India to Thailand
PLANT FAMILY: Orchidaceae
TYPE: Dwarf, deciduous, epiphytic or terrestrial
orchids
USDA ZONE: Z8
MOST SUITED TO: The alpine house

DESCRIPTION: These are near hardy orchids that
are easily battered by wind and weather, so a cold
greenhouse or alpine house is the only place to
grow them successfully. Grow in a good, humus-
rich compost containing plenty of fine grit, and
keep them dry, but never parched, during their
dormant stages. Plants grow from pseudo-bulbs
and foliage can become almost aspidistra-like
when mature. Flowers are white, pink and purple
and all shades between. Many also have yellowish,
greenish or brownish markings. To buy them, you
will need to make contact with specialist alpine
or orchid suppliers.

POPULAR SPECIES AND VARIETIES: *Pleione* naming has
become confused over the past 50 years, and
there are many hybrids available (most derived
from the species *Pleione formosana* AGM).

Potentilla neumanniana 'Nana'

Primula allionii 'Elizabeth Earle'

POTENTILLA (Cinquefoil)

ORIGIN: Throughout the Northern Hemisphere
PLANT FAMILY: Rosaceae
TYPE: Those more suited to the alpine garden are tufted, clumpy or mat-forming perennials
USDA ZONE: Z5
MOST SUITED TO: Rock gardens, sinks, troughs and wall tops

DESCRIPTION: These showy, easy-to-grow plants will succeed in any reasonable soil. Generally regarded as sun-lovers, most will tolerate partial shade. The popular shrubby kinds usually found in garden centres are too large for most rock gardens, but the same open, five-petalled flowers in similar colours are available on the dwarf types as well.

POPULAR SPECIES AND VARIETIES: *Potentilla* x *tonguei* AGM is a long-flowering, mat-forming hybrid with dark green, almost bronzed leaves and carrying masses of soft apricot flowers, suffused with crimson. *P. neumanniana* 'Nana' has lovely golden-yellow flowers. *P. alba* is a tufted plant, just 6in (15cm) high, with white flowers.

PRIMULA

ORIGIN: Most parts of the world (notable exceptions are South Africa and Australasia)
PLANT FAMILY: Primulaceae
TYPE: Mostly cushion- and rosette-forming perennials
USDA ZONE: Z5–8
MOST SUITED TO: Alpine house, rockeries and pots

DESCRIPTION: This is a vast genus that can be divided into several groups, from bog- and moisture-loving types, to woodland and bedding types. There are also sub- and cross-divisions of Asiatic, American and European primulas. In general, the European types have short stems and upward-looking flowers. They are lovers of moist, gritty soils that are leafily organic.

POPULAR SPECIES AND VARIETIES: Of the European types, *Primula allionii* AGM is best suited to the alpine house. It has cushions of 1in (2.5cm) high rosettes of grey-green, short leaves. Of the Asiatic types, *P. chungensis* is a usefully coarse type, grown for its orangey flowers from late spring to early autumn. Of the American types look for *P. suffrutescens*; it is a more shrubby plant, but just 4in (10cm) or so high.

Pulsatilla vulgaris

Ranunculus calandrinioides

PULSATILLA (Pasque flower)

ORIGIN: Mountain slopes throughout Europe, North America and Asia

PLANT FAMILY: Ranunculaceae

TYPE: Hardy perennials

USDA ZONE: Z5

MOST SUITED TO: Sunny rock gardens, screes and containers

DESCRIPTION: The individual flowers of *Pulsatilla* look like clematis or buttercups (all three belong to the same plant family). The blooms of the pasque flower are showy, reddish purple, each with a bold yellow centre, and are accompanied by hairy leaves and silvery seed pods, combining to make a real spectacle in a border or rockery. Plants reach 6–12in (15–30cm) in height.

POPULAR SPECIES AND VARIETIES: Although there are 30 or so named species and cultivars, most are difficult to find. The only species widely available is *Pulsatilla vulgaris* AGM, with bell-shaped flowers of pink-purple. Look out also for 'Alba' AGM (white), 'Barton's Pink' (clear pink), 'Blaue Glocke' (lilac blue), 'Eva Constance' and 'Röde Klokke' (both deep red). *P. vernalis* AGM has intensely hairy leaves, with white flowers; this is better for a frame or alpine house.

RANUNCULUS

ORIGIN: The genus generally can be found throughout the world, but the three alpine species mentioned here are all natives of southern Europe and North Africa

PLANT FAMILY: Ranunculaceae

TYPE: Fibrous and tuberous-rooted perennials

USDA ZONE: Z6–7

MOST SUITED TO: Rock gardens and screes, sinks, troughs, wall tops and the alpine house

DESCRIPTION: Most species flower in spring and early summer and prefer a moist soil; otherwise they are not fussy. The alpine buttercups lack the coarseness of their lowland counterparts, but they often have flowers that are even larger.

POPULAR SPECIES AND VARIETIES: *Ranunculus calandrinioides* AGM is a poppy-like species with grey foliage and flowers up to 2in (5cm) across, held on 6in (15cm) high stems. The colour is pale pink and the stamens are yellow. *R. gramineus* AGM is distinctive for its grassy, grey-green leaves and shining yellow flowers in late spring and early summer. *R. montanus* 'Molten Gold' AGM has a long dormant period, but is covered with yellow blooms in late spring, on 4in (10cm) stalks.

Rhodiola rosea

Rhodohypoxis 'Tetra Red'

RHODIOLA ROSEA (Roseroot)

ORIGIN: Throughout the Northern Hemisphere
PLANT FAMILY: Crassulaceae
TYPE: Thick, fleshy, branching perennials
USDA ZONE: Z1
MOST SUITED TO: Rock gardens and screes, and wall tops

DESCRIPTION: A pleasant plant that has shuffled between being a *Rhodiola* and a *Sedum*, this UK native makes a thick, fleshy rootstock from which rise in spring upright 10in (25cm) high stems carrying many narrow leaves. These stems are tipped by greenish-yellow flowers. It is an attractive plant when 'in season'.

POPULAR SPECIES AND VARIETIES: *Rhodiola heterodonta* is arguably more spectacular; its young stems and leaves are rich purple and the flowers are a deep rust red.

RHODOHYPOXIS

ORIGIN: South Africa
PLANT FAMILY: Hypoxidaceae
TYPE: Stemless perennials, with both fibrous and fleshy roots
USDA ZONE: Z8
MOST SUITED TO: The alpine house and frames

DESCRIPTION: These plants are only suitable for warm, sheltered positions, or for troughs and pans in the alpine house. They are best dried off in winter and kept moist in summer. Most are only 2in (5cm) high when in flower and continue from mid-spring to late summer.

POPULAR SPECIES AND VARIETIES: The so-called red star, *Rhodohypoxis baurii* AGM, is variable, but may be obtained to colour in named cultivars from white (with 'Alba') through to pale pink (with 'Fred Broome') deeper pink (with 'Tetra Red') and others even deeper. *R. baurii* var. *platypetala* has flowers of pure white, occasionally suffused pale pink. *R. milloides* has rose-pink flowers and is probably slightly less hardy. Its cultivar 'Claret' is a much deeper red.

Roscoea humeana AGM

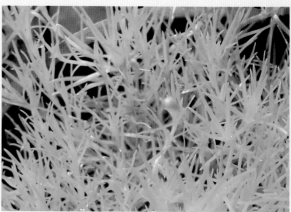

Sagina subulata var. *glabrata* 'Aurea'

ROSCOEA

ORIGIN: China
PLANT FAMILY: Zingiberaceae
TYPE: Rhizomatous perennials
USDA ZONE: Z6–7
MOST SUITED TO: Rock gardens in partial shade

DESCRIPTION: This is a small genus of charming little plants, related to ginger. Their exotic foliage and flowers bring a touch of the tropics to our alpine gardens. You may find them difficult to get hold of, however. These plants do well in woodland rock gardens where they are of considerable value, flowering later than many of the other plants that grow there.

POPULAR SPECIES AND VARIETIES: *Roscoea humeana* AGM is the most robust species with rich green oval leaves and purple flowers from late spring into summer. *R. cautleyoides* AGM has narrow upright leaves and small clusters of usually pale yellow hooded flowers produced in late summer. The cultivar 'Kew Beauty' AGM has flowers of darker yellow. *R. purpurea* has similar rich green foliage and attractive blooms of usually purple, mauve or even white.

SAGINA

ORIGIN: Widespread throughout the temperate regions of the Northern Hemisphere
PLANT FAMILY: Caryophyllaceae
TYPE: Mat-forming, evergreen perennials
USDA ZONE: Z4–5
MOST SUITED TO: Banks, in paving and in walls, rock gardens and the alpine house

DESCRIPTION: This is a small genus of often rather weedy plants. However, there are several desirable plants for the rock garden and alpine house. It is grown mainly for its moss- or fern-like foliage. It dislikes hot, dry soils, but does prefer a sunny spot and a well-drained but moist soil.

POPULAR SPECIES AND VARIETIES: *Sagina boydii* makes a hard cushion of tiny, stiff, bottle-green leaves in small rosettes. It was discovered growing wild in Scotland in 1878, but has never since been seen growing as a wild plant. The flowers are greenish and inconspicuous. *S. subulata* var. *glabrata* 'Aurea' makes low mats of thread-like golden shoots, studded with little white starry flowers in spring.

Saxifraga umbrosa

Saxifraga x megaseiflora 'Josef Kapek'

SAXIFRAGA (Saxifrage)

ORIGIN: Alpine locations in the Northern and Southern Hemisphere, also in many temperate regions, particularly in Asia (but rarely in South America). *Saxifraga* is entirely absent from South Africa and Australia.

PLANT FAMILY: Saxifragaceae

TYPE: Deciduous and evergreen perennials, ranging from tall and leafy-stemmed, to mat- or cushion-formers

USDA ZONE: Z3–7

MOST SUITED TO: All suitable alpine areas

DESCRIPTION: The saxifrage genus is large and important and, rather like the *Primula* genus discussed earlier, deserves a book all to itself. The genus is divided botanically into a number of sections, and within these there are many sub-divisions. Rather than to labour the complex taxonomy of *Saxifraga*, I intend just to list by name the many plants I have succeeded with over the years. Most of the small alpine saxifrages are lime-lovers (although neutral soils are tolerated). They are also sun-lovers, and like the soil to be sharply drained. The principal flowering season is spring and early summer, but there are a few later flowering species.

POPULAR SPECIES AND VARIETIES: The 'mossy' saxifrages are probably the easiest to grow. They form low mounds with sprays of open, bell-shaped flowers in spring. Flower colour varies from white to cream, and many shades of pink through to blood red. *Saxifraga* x *arendsii* 'Triumph' is a good example, with cherry-red flowers on stems 8in (20cm) high.

The cushion-forming saxifrages are often referred to as the Kabschias. These are slow-growers, preferring part-shade and an extremely well-drained soil. *S. burseriana* 'Gloria' AGM is a fabulous white, *S.* x *megasaeflora* 'Josef Kapek' is light pink, *S. megasaeflora* 'Robin Hood' is deep pink, *S.* x *anglica* 'Winifred' a medium red, *S.* x *boydii* 'Faldonside' is a lemon yellow, and *S.* 'Tysoe' is primrose yellow. All flower from late winter to mid-spring.

The encrusted or Aizoon saxifrages make rosettes mostly silvered, varying in size from less than ½in (1cm) across to 8in (20cm) or more. These are easier to grow outdoors. *S. paniculata* 'Lutea' AGM is light yellow. *S. cochlearis* 'Minor' AGM is white, while the magnificent 'Tumbling Waters' AGM is white on long arching sprays of flowers. (Continued on page 148.)

Saxifraga 'Tysoe'

Scilla mischtschenkoana AGM

SAXIFRAGA (Saxifrage) continued from page 147

Then there are the larger-leaved and larger plants, such as 'London Pride' (*S. umbrosa*). Cabbage-like rosettes of evergreen, leathery, spoon-shaped leaves are produced on strawberry-like runners. Tall flower stems are produced and in late spring these carry a mist of white or pink flowers. The plant commonly known as mother-of-thousands (*S. stolonifera*) is often grown as a house plant, but it will in fact grow outside in sheltered positions, where it will form an attractive spreading plant over rock, its evergreen oval leaves spreading freely. The hybrid *S.* 'Stansfieldii' produces lovely rose-pink flowers with yellow-green centres. *S. fortunei* is a leafy plant rather similar in appearance to a *Heuchera*, but the foliage is glossier and somewhat succulent in appearance. Dainty white, star-shaped blooms are carried in airy masses on long stems in late autumn. The variety 'Black Ruby' has almost black leaves and pink flowers.

SCILLA MISCHTSCHENKOANA AGM (Squill)

ORIGIN: Russia, Iran
PLANT FAMILY: Hyacinthaceae
TYPE: Bulbous perennials
USDA ZONE: Z5–6
MOST SUITED TO: The alpine house and sheltered sinks and troughs

DESCRIPTION: Between mid-winter and mid-spring these plants produce a veritable carpet of pale blue; there is a deeper blue stripe on each petal. It grows to 6in (15cm) in height and, like so many bulbs, is best planted in groups.

POPULAR SPECIES AND VARIETIES: *Scilla siberica* AGM has lovely blue, nodding flowers and is the loveliest and easiest species; its leaves make their appearance in early spring and are soon followed by the 4in (10cm) stems carrying the bell-shaped flowers. *S. sibirica* 'Spring Beauty' is a robust form with larger bright blue flowers. 'Alba' is a good white flowering variety. The dainty *S. bifolia* AGM produces two strap-shaped leaves that open out to allow a 4in (10cm) high stem, holding blue star-shaped flowers, in late winter. 'Rosea' is a purple-pink form and 'Alba' is white. *S. verna* has electric-blue flowers in spring.

Sedum rupestre 'Angelina'

Sedum spathulifolium 'Cape Blanco' AGM

SEDUM (Stonecrop)

ORIGIN: Northern temperate and tropical mountain regions

PLANT FAMILY: Crassulaceae

TYPE: Clump- and mat-forming succulents and perennials

USDA ZONE: Z5–9

MOST SUITED TO: Rock gardens, sinks, troughs, wall tops and sides, and the alpine house

DESCRIPTION: This is another immense genus of plants, and only a relatively small selection are true alpines. With one or two exceptions, all sedums are sun-loving plants, and the majority of them thrive in the poorest of soils. Most gardeners will be familiar with the so-called iceplant sedums, which are best suited to general flower and mixed borders. These are generally too large for rock gardens. The common name of stonecrop applies actually to only one species, *Sedum acre*. Some alpine enthusiasts would not consider growing it as it can be a thug when grown with choicer plants. Fortunately there are many other species and cultivars worthy of a place on the rock garden and in the alpine house.

POPULAR SPECIES AND VARIETIES: *Sedum ewersii* has near-prostrate growth with glaucous leaves and heads of pink flowers on 6in (15cm) high stems in mid-summer. *S. kamtschaticum* var. *floriferum* 'Weihenstephaner Gold' makes a fine show of deep yellow above dense green leaves from early summer onwards. *S. middendorffianum* is also deep yellow and more compact, at 4in (10cm). The purple-green-leaved *S. oreganum* are lower at 3in (7.5cm), and the powdery, grey-purple, mounded forms of *S. spathulifolium* are lower still at just 2in (5cm). Of this latter species the cultivar 'Cape Blanco' AGM is ubiquitous, with its whitish-grey leaves and small golden-yellow summer flowers. *S. rupestre* is a European species forming low mats of tangled stems and rather blue-grey leaves and cymes of yellow flowers. The cultivar 'Angelina' is a form with distinctly gold-green foliage. *S. spurium* makes non-invasive, spreading carpets with flowers in shades of pink and red on 3–4in (7.5–10cm) high stalks. Look for the cultivars 'Ruby Mantle' and 'Purpurteppich', both of which have purplish leaves all year round.

Sempervivum 'Blood Tip'

Sempervivum 'Corona'

SEMPERVIVUM (Houseleek)

ORIGIN: Europe, North Africa and western Asia

PLANT FAMILY: Crassulaceae

TYPE: Low, rosette-forming perennials

USDA ZONE: Z4–8

MOST SUITED TO: Containers, rock gardens, the alpine house – and house roofs, (which has gained them a reputation and a common name)

DESCRIPTION: The houseleek offers a solution for those who want to grow succulent plants but are worried about hardiness. The Latin name means 'always alive' and to prove this, the genus is tolerant of cold, draughts, poor soil conditions as well as drought. Plants are considered very hardy, although they are not tolerant of prolonged wet conditions, doing best in a well-drained, gritty soil. If planted in a sink or trough, it is recommended that they are brought inside and kept in a cool, dry area during the winter. The plants provide a wide range of leaf rosette colours, from green, through pink and brown to dark purple-black. Flowers are produced at the end of long stalks that appear in the second or third year. The star-shaped blooms are pink, purple, yellow or white. After flowering, the rosette will die off, leaving a

space that can be filled by another rosette. The genus is very close to the related genera of *Jovibarba* and *Rosularia*. I maintain that all three genera should be entirely separate, although many growers and enthusiasts lump them together.

POPULAR SPECIES AND VARIETIES: With more than 40 species and some 1,000 named cultivars, the gardener is spoilt for choice. There are so many named forms it is impossible to say which is best, and many nurserymen sell the same plant under different names. Hybridization is common and often plants grown from seed are not true to type, but growing from offsets ensures uniformity. Many forms are sold by leaf colour and without a name, but some worth searching for are *Sempervivum* 'Amanda' (a fast grower with dark purple-brown, long tapering leaves), 'Apple Blossom' (medium-sized, open rosettes of apple green, with shades of pink in full sun), 'Black Prince' (purplish black in summer; the leaves are edged with silvery hairs), 'Corona' (deep green with attractive maroon shading on the inner parts of the leaves), and 'Blood Tip'

Sempervivum arachnoideum AGM

Silene acaulis subsp. *acaulis*

SILENE (Campion)

ORIGIN: Throughout the Northern Hemisphere and South Africa
PLANT FAMILY: Caryophyllaceae
TYPE: Tufted or mat-forming perennials
USDA ZONE: Z2–5
MOST SUITED TO: All suitable alpine areas

DESCRIPTION: These are normally easy-to-grow, clump-forming meadow plants and survive in any well-drained soil (although the moss campion, *Silene acaulis*, sometimes grows in quite damp places in the wild). They have five-petalled, somewhat *Dianthus*-like flowers (the two plants belong to the same family), which generally appear in spring and early summer.

POPULAR SPECIES AND VARIETIES: *Silene acaulis* subsp. *acaulis* puts on a bright display of small, clear pink flowers. *S. alpestris* forms deep green tufts and sends up 8in (20cm) sprays of white flowers. 'Flore Pleno' AGM is the double form of this. *S. schafta* AGM produces bright pink flowers from mid-summer until early autumn.

(large, compact rosettes of pale green to olive green; striking bronze tinted leaves with dark red or scarlet tips; they are blood red in winter). *S. arachnoideum* AGM produces red flowers, but its main attraction is the cobweb-like strands that link the leaf tips. It's always a talking point. *S. calcareum* 'Mrs Giuseppi' is a very neat plant with bright green rosettes, and bright red leaf tips. I particularly like *S. calcareum* 'Extra'; it produces large, symmetrical, many-leaved rosettes. The leaves are bluish-green with very distinct, dark brownish-red tips. A stylish cultivar is 'Director Jacobs', with large, symmetrical rosettes comprising many short, wide leaves. It is deep red and silver.

Sisyrinchium 'Californian Skies'

Sternbergia greuteriana

SISYRINCHIUM

ORIGIN: North and South America
PLANT FAMILY: Iridaceae
TYPE: Grass-like, clump-forming perennials
USDA ZONE: Z3–8
MOST SUITED TO: Rock gardens and screes

DESCRIPTION: These are not difficult plants to grow, and they have a long flowering season. When in leaf they resemble miniature, grassy leaved irises, but the flowers are simple and open, making up for their lack of size by shear quantity. Many sisyrinchiums will self-sow readily, so lots of plants may emanate from one bought-in specimen. Whereas this can be welcome, it can also be a nuisance as they can spread all over the rock garden.

POPULAR SPECIES AND VARIETIES: *Sisyrinchium idahoense* var. *bellum* and *S. angustifolium* (known as blue-eyed grass) have deep blue flowers on 6in (15cm) long stems. *S. californicum* Brachypus Group is yellow and the cultivar named 'Mrs Spivey' is white. 'Californian Skies' is pale blue with deeper centres and yellow stamens.

STERNBERGIA (Autumn daffodil)

ORIGIN: Turkey; eastwards towards Kashmir, and westwards towards Spain
PLANT FAMILY: Amaryllidaceae
TYPE: Bulbous perennials
USDA ZONE: Z5–7
MOST SUITED TO: The alpine house, sheltered containers and pockets on the rock garden

DESCRIPTION: The flowers look like a type of *Crocus*, but in fact the *Sternbergia* belongs to the *Narcissus* family. Nearly all forms produce yellow flowers (or shades thereof), with a few whites. Most flower in early to mid-autumn, but of course there are always exceptions.

POPULAR SPECIES AND VARIETIES: *Sternbergia lutea* produces strap-like, dark green leaves, rather like small daffodils, appearing before the flowers. The flowers are bright golden yellow, held low to the ground. *S. sicula* is probably only a variety of *S. lutea* with narrower leaves, but is possibly freer flowering. *S. candida* is a choice late-winter-flowering species with snow-white flowers; *S. greuteriana* is similar but deep yellow.

Tanacetum haradjanii

Thymus pulegioides 'Archer's Gold'

TANACETUM

ORIGIN: Europe, North Africa, Asia and North America
PLANT FAMILY: Asteraceae
TYPE: Clump-forming or branched perennials, or sub-shrubs
USDA ZONE: Z7–8
MOST SUITED TO: Rock gardens or screes, wall tops and raised beds

DESCRIPTION: These are very aromatic plants. *Tanacetum* is a sizeable genus and it includes the fragrant herb tansy; however, very few species are of interest to the alpine gardener. But there are one or two good plants, grown mainly for their attractive foliage. They like full sun and well-drained soil.

POPULAR SPECIES AND VARIETIES: *Tanacetum haradjanii*, originally from Turkey and Syria, is a tufted plant with dissected silver foliage and large, white, daisy-like flowers. Very similar is *T. densum* subsp. *amani*.

THYMUS (Thyme)

ORIGIN: The Mediterranean region and western Asia
PLANT FAMILY: Lamiaceae
TYPE: Creeping, mat- and bush-forming sub-shrubs and small shrubs
USDA ZONE: Z5–9
MOST SUITED TO: Rock gardens, screes, wall tops, sinks and troughs

DESCRIPTION: Most familiar as the culinary herb thyme, there are several species that are perfectly at home on the rock garden; those with aromatic foliage can still be used in cuisine.

POPULAR SPECIES AND VARIETIES: The true, lemon-scented *Thymus citriodorus* is bush-forming at 6in (15cm) in height. However, the straight green-leaved types are unworthy when there are gold ('Golden Queen'), silver ('Silver Queen' AGM) and variegated ('Variegatus') forms from which to choose. *T. pulegioides* has small flower heads of mauve, white or crimson. There are many excellent cultivars of it including 'Archer's Gold' (variegated yellow and green leaves) and 'Bertram Anderson' AGM (deep green leaves and a long display of lavender-mauve flowers).

Tiarella cordifolia AGM

Uvularia grandiflora AGM

TIARELLA (Foamflower)

ORIGIN: North America
PLANT FAMILY: Saxifragaceae
TYPE: Rhizomatous perennials
USDA ZONE: Z3
MOST SUITED TO: Shaded rock gardens, screes and wall tops

DESCRIPTION: Tiarellas are cultivated chiefly for their clumps of handsome foliage, rather like small *Heuchera*. However, from late spring onwards short spikes of little frothy pink-white flowers appear. It will only form a good thick, bushy growth if the soil is moist and fertile. It will tolerate quite deep shade, and in fact is nowhere near as good when grown in full sun.

POPULAR SPECIES AND VARIETIES: *Tiarella cordifolia* AGM carries evergreen heart-shaped leaves, each with 3–5 shallow lobes and faintly streaked, striped or mottled scarlet to maroon, or plain green. White to pale pink flowers are carried in upright spikes in spring. *T. wherryi* is the species most often seen in cultivation. It has starry flowers of the palest pink.

UVULARIA GRANDIFLORA AGM (Merry bells)

ORIGIN: North America
PLANT FAMILY: Convallariaceae
TYPE: Rhizomatous perennials
USDA ZONE: Z5
MOST SUITED TO: Lightly shaded rock gardens, screes and wall tops

DESCRIPTION: These woodland perennials really should be grown more widely. Their dainty, pale yellow, dangling, bell-shaped flowers have long, twisted petals and hang from slender, rather arching stems that reach only 12in (30cm) or less in height. They appear in mid- to late spring. The leaves are narrow, oval and greyish green. The plant will not thrive if grown in a container as it needs a free root run and cooler soil conditions than are generally achieved in pot-growing.

POPULAR SPECIES AND VARIETIES: *Uvularia grandiflora* AGM is the most commonly seen variety, but U. *grandiflora* var. *pallida* with its even paler yellow blooms is worth a try. *U. sessilifolia* is the smallest species with pale yellow to straw-coloured flowers in late spring and early summer.

Viola labradorica

Zauschneria californica subsp. *garrettii*

VIOLA (Violet)

ORIGIN: Worldwide; some forms found in the tropics, yet others in the Arctic region

PLANT FAMILY: Violaceae

TYPE: Clump-forming, often spreading and seeding perennials

USDA ZONE: Z3–4

MOST SUITED TO: Rock gardens, wall tops and containers

DESCRIPTION: These well-loved plants may not be true alpines, but some are certainly worth including. The leaves of all forms of *Viola* are loosely heart-shaped, in many cases enlarging once the showy spring flowering has finished. Most enjoy full sun, but *Viola cornuta* AGM and *V. cucullata* prefer dappled shade.

POPULAR SPECIES AND VARIETIES: *Viola cornuta* AGM (the horned violet) is quite a spreader, and has a long succession of light blue 'horned', pansy flowers. *V. cornuta* 'Alba Minor' has white flowers. *V. cucullata* AGM is known as the marsh blue violet, the flowers being held well above the leaves. The Labrador violet (*V. labradorica*) is a deciduous clump-former, with violet-blue spring flowers.

ZAUSCHNERIA CALIFORNICA (Californian fuchsia)

ORIGIN: California and Mexico

PLANT FAMILY: Onagraceae

TYPE: Clump-forming sub-shrubs

USDA ZONE: Z8

MOST SUITED TO: Rock and scree gardens, raised beds and wall tops

DESCRIPTION: This is a sparsely branched sub-shrub with small but long, willow-like leaves and clusters of tubular scarlet flowers some 1in (2.5cm) or more in length. The flowers are at their best in late summer and early autumn, but odd flowers also appear at other times. The plant is slightly tender, but will survive most winters except in the coldest areas. It is useful for providing an intense red flower colour at a time when hardly any other flowers of this colour exist (with the exception, I suppose, of the red *Schizostylis* bulb found in some mixed borders).

POPULAR SPECIES AND VARIETIES: *Zauschneria californica* subsp. *cana* is similar to the species, but has narrower, silver-haired foliage. *Z. septentrionalis* has a more dwarf and tufted habit.

GLOSSARY

Alpine house
An unheated greenhouse used for the growing of mainly alpine and bulbous plants, which provides greater ventilation and usually more light than a conventional greenhouse.

Bract
A modified or reduced leaf, generally set adjacent to the stalk of a flower or the flower itself.

Bulbil
A small bulb produced on the stem or in a leaf axil (or in the flower itself).

Bulblet
A small bulb produced from the existing bulb.

Calcareous
Chalky; containing or resembling calcium carbonate.

Corm
A globular stem base, swollen with food and surrounded by papery scale leaves.

Cultivar
A cultivated plant clearly distinguished by one or more characteristics and which retains these characteristics when propagated; a contraction of 'cultivated variety', and often abbreviated to 'cv.' in plant naming.

Cyme(s)
Inflorescence in which the first flower is the terminal bud of the main stem, with subsequent flowers developing as terminal buds on side shoots or lateral stems.

Epiphyte/Epiphytic
A plant that in nature grows on the surface of another without being parasitic.

Genus (pl. Genera)
A category in plant naming, comprising a group of related species.

Glabrous
Smooth, with a covering of fine hairs.

Glaucous
Covered with grayish, wax-like bloom.

Hybrid
The offspring of genetically different parents, usually produced in cultivation, but occasionally arising in the wild.

Inflorescence
A cluster of flowers with a distinct arrangement.

Mulch
Layer of material applied to the soil surface, to conserve moisture, improve its structure, protect roots from frost, and suppress weeds.

Perennial
Plant that lives for at least three seasons.

pH scale
A scale measured from 1–14 that indicates the alkalinity or acidity of soil. pH 7 is neutral; pH 1–7 is acid, pH 7–14 is alkaline.

Procumbent
Trailing or resting on the ground.

Raceme
Many individual flowers forming an inflorescence, each flower on its own stalk.

Rhizome/Rhizomatous
A stem formation at or below ground level; plants with this trait.

Rootball
The roots and surrounding soil or compost visible when a plant is removed from a pot.

Scree
An area composed of a deep layer of stone chippings mixed with a small amount of soil. It provides extremely sharp drainage for plants that resent moisture at their base.

Sideshoot
A stem that arises from the side of a main shoot or stem.

Single
A single layer of petals opening out into a fairly flat shape, comprising no more than five petals.

Species
A category in plant naming, the rank below genus, containing related, individual plants.

Sub-shrub
A plant that is woody at the base although the upper shoots die back in winter.

Sucker
Generally a shoot that arises from below ground, emanating from a plant's roots, but also refers to any shoot on a grafted plant that originates from below the graft union.

Terrestrial
Growing on the ground with roots in soil (usually used in reference to orchids and bromeliads which may sometimes be terrestrial, or epiphytic).

Tuber/Tuberous
A thickened, usually underground, storage organ derived from a stem or root; plants grown from tubers.

Variety
Botanically, a naturally occurring variant of a wild species; usually shortened to 'var.' in plant naming.

INDEX

Illustrations of plants are shown in **bold**.

A

Acantholimon 104
  glumaceum 104
  ulicinum **104**
Acorus (sweet flag or sweet rush) 104
  gramineus 104
    'Oborozuki' **104**
    'Ogon' 104
    var. *pusillus* 104
    'Variegatus' 104
Aethionema 105
  grandiflorum 105
  'Warley Rose' **105**
  'Warley Ruber' 105
Ajuga (bugle) 93, 105
  reptans
    'Braunherz' 105
    'Burgundy Glow' 105
    'Catlin's Giant' 105
    'Variegata' **105**
Allium (ornamental onion) 106
  cyaneum 106
  flavum **106**
  flavum subsp. *flavum* var. *minus* 106
  insubricum 106
  karataviense **106**
  mairei var. *amabile* 106
  moly 106
  oreophilum 106
  oreophilum 'Zwanenburg' 106
  sphaerocephalon 106
alpine balsam **123**
alpine houses 26, 63–72, 156
  cleaning 94
  displaying alpines 68–9
  heating 72
  shading 71
  siting 67
  ventilation 70
alpine plants
  groups 14–17
  origins 10–12
Andromeda 83
  polifolia (marsh andromeda) 107
    'Compacta' **107**
    'Compacta Alba' 107
Androsace 96, 107
  alpina 107
  'Millstream' **107**
  vandellii 107

Anemone 91, 108
  blanda 108
    'Radar' 108
    'White Splendour' 108
  ranunculoides **108**
aphids 77
Arabis 91, 108
  alpina subsp. *caucasica* 108
    'Variegata' **103**
  'Corfe Castle' 108
  ferdinandi-coburgii 108
  'Old Gold' **108**
  'Rosea' 108
  'Schneehaube' 108
Armeria (thrift or sea pink) 109
  juniperifolia 'Bevan's Variety' **109**
  maritima 109
    'Alba' 109
Aubrieta 17, 39, 109
  'Aureovariegata' 109
  deltoidea 'Doctor Mules' **109**
  'Red Carpet' 109
Aurinia saxatilis (rock garden alyssum) **110**
  'Citrina' 110
  'Compacta' 110
  'Dudley Nevill' 110
  'Flore Pleno' 110
autumn crocus **115**
autumn daffodil **152**
avens **128**

B

beard tongue (*Penstemon*) 16, **141**
bellflower 16, **112**
bindweed 40, **116**
bishop's mitre (*Epimedium*) 51, **122**
bugle **105**
bulbs
  buying 89
  planting 90
  repotting 88

C

Californian fuchsia **155**
Callirhoe involucrata (purple poppy mallow) **110**
Calluna vulgaris (heather) 111
  'Corbett's Red' 111
  'Golden Turret' 111
  'Liebestraum' **111**
Campanula (bellflower) 16, 83, 91, 112
  arvatica 112
  carpatica **112**
  fragilis 112
  media (Canterbury bells) 91
campion **151**
Canterbury bells 91
carnations (*Dianthus*) 21, 39, 91, **120**
cascades 49
Cassiope 20

caves and grottos 46
Cerastium (mouse-ear chickweed) 112
  alpinum 112
    var. *lanatum* 112
  tomentosum 93, **112**
Chamaecyparis (false cypress) 113
  'Gnome' 113
  'Green Globe' 113
  lawsoniana 'Aurea Densa' 113
  'Minima Glauca' 113
  obtusa
    'Kosteri' 113
    'Nana' **113**
  pisifera 'Nana' **113**
Chamaemelum nobile (chamomile) **24**, 114
  'Flore Pleno' 114
  'Treneague' **114**
chamomile **24**, **114**
Chiastophyllum oppositifolium 114
  'Frosted Jade/ Jim's Pride' **114**
cinquefoil **143**
clump-formers 16–17
Colchicum 115
  autumnale (autumn crocus) 115
    'Alboplenum' 115
    'Album' 115
  boissieri **115**
  byzantinum 115
  cupanii **115**
  speciosum 115
    'Atrorubens' 115
    'Waterlily' 115
compost 39
containers 25, 55–61
  compost for 60
  hypertufa 58–9
  planting 60
  plunging 68, 69
  sinks 25, 56–7, 59
  siting 59
Convolvulus (bindweed) 40, **116**
  cneorum 116
  lineatus 116
Cornus (dogwood) 116
  canadensis **116**
  'Eddie's White Wonder' 116
  florida 116
cranesbill (*Geranium*) 33, **128**
Crepis (hawk's beard) 117
  aurea 117
  incana **117**
  'Pink Mist' 117
Crocus 45, 91, 117–18
  'Ard Schenk' **117**, 118
  Chysanthus Group 118
    'Blue Pearl' 118
    'Cream Beauty' 118
    'E.P. Bowles' 118
    'Snow Bunting' 118

kotschyanus 118
'Pickwick' 118
'Queen of the Blues' 118
sativus 118
sieberi subsp. *sublimis* 'Tricolor' 118
speciosus subsp. *xantholaimos* **118**
tommasinianus 118
'Ruby Giant' 118
'Whitewell Purple' 118
'Vanguard' 118
cuttings 83, 85, 90
Cyclamen 20, 77, 118–19
cilicium 119
cilicium f. *album* 119
coum 119
graecum **118**, 119
hederifolium 119
mirabile 119
purpurascens **119**
repandum 119
Cypripedium calceolus pubescens
(lady's slipper orchid) 96

D
daffodil (*Narcissus*) 89, 90, 91, 96, **138**
Daphne 119
bholua 'Jacqueline Postill' 119
x *napolitana* **119**
odora 119
'Aureomarginata' 119
Delphinium 120
brunonianum 120
grandiflorum 120
muscosum 120
nudicaule 'Laurin' **120**
Dianthus (carnations and pinks) 21, 39, 91, 120
alpinus 120
deltoides **120**
'Joan's Blood' 120
Dionysia 121
aretioides 121
bryoides 121
curviflora **121**
Dodecatheon (shooting stars) 121
dentatum 121
meadia **29, 121**
pulchellum subsp. *cusickii* 121
dogwood **116**

E
edelweiss **135**
Epimedium (Bishop's mitre) 51, 122
alpinum 122
grandiflorum 'Mount Kitadake' **122**
Eranthis (winter aconite) 34
Erica (ling and heather) 111
carnea 111
'King George' **111**
'Ruby Glow' 111

erigena 111
'Golden Lady' 111
'W.T. Rackliff' 111
vagans 111
'Mrs D.F. Maxwell' 111
'Valerie Proudley' 111
Erigeron (fleabane) 122
glaucus 122
karvinskianus **122**
'Sea Breeze' 122
Erinus alpinus (alpine balsam) 123
var. *albus* **123**
'Doktor Hähle' 123
'Mrs Charles Boyle' 123
Eriogonum (wild buckwheat)
kennedyi var. *alpigenum* **16, 123**
wrightii var. *subscaposum* 123
Erodium (storksbill) 83, 124
corsicum **124**
x. *variabile* 124
'Bishop's Form' 124
'Flore Pleno' 124
Erysimum (wallflower) 91
Euonymus
fortunei
'Emerald Gaiety' 124
'Emerald 'n' Gold' 124
'Silver Queen' 124
japonicus 124
'Microphyllus Aureovariagatus' **124**
Euphorbia
characias 125
mysinites (spurge) **125**
polychroma 125
evening primrose **139**

F
false cypress **113**
feeding 79
fertilizer 79
fescue **125**
Festuca (fescue) 125
glauca 125
'Blaufuchs' 125
rubra 125
flax **136**
fleabane **122**
foamflower **154**
forget-me-not 91
fountains 49

G
Galanthus
elwesii 126
ikariae 126
nivalis (common snowdrop) **34**, 126
'Flore Pleno' 126
'Lady Elphinstone' 126
'Magnet' **126**

'Merlin' **126**
'S. Arnott' 126
'Virdapicis' 126
Gaultheria 20
Gentiana (gentian) 60, 127
acaulis 127
asclepiadea 127
makinoi 'Marsha' 127
septemfida 127
sino-ornata 127
'Strathmore' **127**
verna **127**
Geranium (cranesbill) 33, 128
cinereum 128
'Laurence Flatman' **128**
sanguineum 128
var. *striatum* 128
Geum (avens) 128
montanum 128
reptans 128
'Borisii' **128**
gravel 40, 45, 82
greenhouses 26–7, 65, 66
see also alpine houses
Gypsophila 16

H
Haberlea 20
ferdinandi-coburgii 129
rhodopensis **129**
'Virginalis' 129
Hacquetia epipactis **129**
'Thor' 129
hawk's beard **117**
heather 11, 39, **76**, **111**
Hebe 130
albicans 130
x *andersonii* 'Andersonii Variegata' **130**
armstrongii 130
buchananii 130
'Emerald Gem' **130**
ochracea 'James Stirling' 130
pinguifolia 'Pagei' 130
'Youngii' 130
Helianthemum (sun rose or rock rose) 16, 131
'Ben Fahda' 131
'Ben Heckla' 131
'Ben Macdhui' 131
'Ben Nevis' 131
'Rhodanthe Carneum' **131**
'Wisley Primrose' 131
Hepatica 131
nobilis 131
var. *japonica* **131**
transsilvanica 131
herbaceous alpines 17
high altitude plants 15
Himalayas 10, 96
houseleak (*Sempervivum*) 21, **24**, 96, **150–1**

Hypericum (St John's wort) 132
    balearicum 132
    calycinum 132
    coris 132
    olympicum **132**
hypertufa
    containers 58–9
    for covering sinks 57

I
Iberis (perennial candytuft) 16, 83, 132
    saxatilis **132**
    sempervirens 132
Indian crocus 142
Iris 133
    histrioides
        'Major' 133
    reticulata 45
        'Harmony' 133
        'Katherine Hodgkin' 133
        'Pauline' **133**

J
Jeffersonia 133
    diphylla 133
    dubia **133**
Juniperus
    communis (common juniper) 134
        'Brynhyfryd Gold' 134
        'Compressa' **134**
        'Green Carpet' 134
        'Miniatur' 134
    horizontalis 'Blue Pygmy' 134

L
Lachenalia
    aloides (leopard lily) 134
        contaminata 134
        var. *quadricolor* **134**
        viridiflora 134
lady's slipper orchid 96
leaf cuttings 84
Leontopodium
    alpinum (edelweiss) 135
    kamtschaticum **135**
    souliei 135
leopard lily **134**
Leptinella 135
    atrata 135
        subsp. *luteola* 135
    squalida 'Platt's Black' **135**
Lewisia cotyledon Ashwood strain **136**
Lilium 96
ling 111
Linum (flax) 136
    arboreum 136
    flavum 136
    'Gemmell's Hybrid' 136
    narbonense **136**

Lithodora 137
    'Grace Ward' 137
    'Heavenly Blue' **137**

M
mail order 30–1
marsh andromeda **107**
Massonia 137
    echinata **137**
    pustulata 137
mat-forming alpines 16–17
mature rock garden 14
Meconopsis 96
merry bells **154**
mouse-ear chickweed 93, **112**
mulches 82, 86, 157
Muscari 45
Myosotis arvensis (forget-me-not) 91

N
Narcissus (daffodil) 89, 90, 91, 96, 138
    bulbocodium 138
    cantabricus **138**
    'February Gold' 138
    'Rip Van Winkle' 138
    romieuxii subsp. *romieuxii* **138**
    'Tete-a-Tete' 138
Nierembergia repens (*rivularis*) **139**

O
Oenothera (evening primrose) 139
    caespitosa **139**
    macrocarpa 139
Origanum 140
    calcaratum 140
    dictamnus 140
    x *hybridinum* 140
    majorana 140
    vulgare 'Aureum' **140**
ornamental onion **106**
Oxalis (sorrel or shamrock) 140
    acetosella 140
        var. *rosea* 140
    laciniata 140
    melanosticta **140**

P
pasque flower (*Pulsatilla*) 91, **144**
peat block gardens 51
Penstemon (beard tongue) 16, 141
    hirsutus var. *pygmaea* **141**
    laetus subsp. *roezlii* 141
    pinifolius 141
    'Mersea Yellow' 141
perennial candytuft (*Iberis*) 16, 83, **132**
pest control 77, 78
Phlox 141
    divaricata subsp. *laphamii*
        'Chattahoochee' **141**

douglasii 141
    'Apollo' 141
    'Boothman's Variety' 141
    'Crackerjack' 141
    'Iceberg' 141
    sublata 141
Picea (spruce) 142
    abies 'Elegans' **142**
    pungens Glauca Group 142
pinks (*Dianthus*) 21, 39, 91, **120**
planting
    bulbs 90
    in containers 60
    new alpines 80
    on rockery banks 44–5
    in tufa gardens 52, 53
plastic containers 59
Pleione (Indian crocus) **142**
ponds 48–9, 50
Potentilla (cinquefoil) 143
    alba 143
    neumanniana 'Nana' **143**
    x *tonguei* 143
Primula 20, 51, 60, 77, 91, 143
    allioni **31**
        'Elizabeth Earle' **143**
    chungensis 143
    suffrutescens 143
Pulsatilla (pasque flower) 91, 144
    vernalis 144
    vulgaris **144**
        'Alba' 144
        'Barton's Pink' 144
        'Blaue Glocke' 144
        'Röde Klokke' 144
purple poppy mallow **110**
Pyrenees 96

R
raised beds 22
Ramonda 20, 51
Ranunculus 96, 144
    calandrinioides **144**
    gramineus 144
    montanus 'Molten Gold' 144
Rhodiola
    heterodonta 145
    rosea (roseroot) **145**
Rhododendron 3, **86**
Rhodohypoxis 145
    baurii 145
        'Alba' 145
        'Fred Broome' 145
        var. *platypetala* 145
        'Tetra Red' **145**
    milloides 145
        'Claret' 145
rock garden alyssum **110**
rock rose (*Helianthemum*) 16, **131**

rockeries/rock gardens 6, 12–13, 20, 21
   building 38–40, 77
   structure 40
   with water features 48–50
   see also caves and grottos; peat block
      gardens; rockery banks; tufa gardens
rockery banks 42–5
Roscoea 146
   cautleyoides 146
   humeana **146**
   'Kew Beauty' 146
   purpurea 146
roseroot **145**

S
Sagina 146
   boydii 146
   subulata var. glabrata 'Aurea' **146**
St John's wort **132**
Saponaria 21
Saxifraga (saxifrage) 21, 83, 91, 147–8
   angelica 'Winifred' 147
   x arendsii 147
   boydii 'Faldonside' 147
   burseriana 'Gloria' 147
   cochlearis
      'Minor' 147
      'Tumbling Waters' 147
   fortunei
      'Black Ruby' 148
   'London Pride' 148
   x megaseiflora 'Josef Kapek' **17**, **147**
   x megaseiflora 'Robin Hood' 147
   paniculata 'Lutea' 147
   'Stansfieldii' 148
   stolonifera 148
   'Tysoe' **148**
   umbrosa **147**
Scilla (squill) 148
   'Alba' 148
   bifolia
      'Alba' 148
      'Rosea' 148
   mischtschenkoana **148**
   sibirica 148
   sibirica 'Spring Beauty' 148
   verna 148
scree plants 15
sea pink **109**
Sedum (stonecrop) 21, 96, 149
   acre 149
   ewersii 149
   kamtschaticum var. floriferum
      'Weihenstephaner Gold' 149

middendorffianum 149
oreganum 149
rupestre 'Angelina' **149**
spathulifolium 'Cape Blanco' **149**
spurium 149
   'Purpurteppich' 149
   'Ruby Mantle' 149
Sempervivum (houseleek) 21, **24**, 96, 150–1
   'Amanda' 150
   'Apple Blossom' 150
   arachnoideum **151**
   'Black Prince' 150
   'Blood Tip' **150**
   calcareum
      'Director Jacobs' 151
      'Extra' 151
      'Mrs Giuseppi' 151
   'Corona' **150**
shading 84
shamrock **140**
shooting stars (Dodecatheon) **29**, **121**
Silene (campion) 151
   acaulis subsp. acaulis **151**
   alpestris 151
      'Flore Pleno' 151
   schafta 151
sinks 25, 56–7, 59
Sisyrinchium 152
   angustifolium 152
   'Californian Skies' **152**
   idahoense var. bellum 152
   'Mrs Spivey' 152
slate chippings 15, 60, 82
slate gardens 21
snowdrop **34**, **45**, **126**
Soldanella 96
sorrel **140**
sowing seeds 80, 91
spruce **142**
spurge **125**
squill **148**
Sternbergia (autumn daffodil) 152
   candida 152
   greuteriana **152**
   lutea 152
   sicula 152
stonecrop (Sedum) 21, 96, **149**
storksbill (Erodium) 83, **124**
sun rose (Helianthemum) 16, **131**
sweet flag **104**
sweet rush **104**

T
Tanacetum 153
   densum subsp. amani 153
   haradjanii **153**
thrift **109**
Thymus (thyme) 83, 153
   citriodorus 153
   'Golden Queen' 153
   pulegioides 153
      'Archer's Gold' **153**
      'Bertram Anderson' 153
   'Silver Queen' 153
   'Variegatus' 153
Tiarella (foamflower) 154
   cordifolia **154**
   wherryi 154
troughs 56, 57
tufa gardens 52–3
tufa rock 26
tufa rock walls 23

U
Uvularia (merry bells) 154
   grandiflora **154**
      var. pallida 154
   sessilifolia 154

V
Vaccinium 20, 51
Veronica 83
Viola 96
Viola (violet) 155
   cornuta 155
      'Alba Minor' 155
   cucullata 155
   labradorica **155**

W
wallflower 91
water features 48–50
waterfalls 48, 49
   maintenance 94
watering 82, 86, 89
weeds 40, 81, 87
wild buckwheat (Erigonum) **16**, **123**
winter aconite 34

Z
Zauschneria
   californica (Californian fuchsia) 155
      subsp. garrettii **17**, **155**
   septentrionalis 155

GMC Publications Ltd, 166 High Street, Lewes, East Sussex,
BN7 1XU, United Kingdom
Tel: 01273 488005 Fax: 01273 402866
www.gmcbooks.com

Contact us for a complete catalogue, or visit our website.